MAGISTERIUM

■ ■ ■

Teacher and Guardian of the Faith

INTRODUCTIONS TO CATHOLIC DOCTRINE

This series provides readable scholarly introductions to key themes in Catholic doctrine, written by preeminent scholars from around the world. The volumes of the series are suitable for college, university, and seminary courses, as well as for educated readers of all ages who seek to grow in their understanding of the Catholic faith.

■ ■ ■

PUBLISHED VOLUMES

Avery Cardinal Dulles, SJ, *Magisterium, Teacher and Guardian of the Faith*
Daniel A. Keating, *Deification and Grace*
Steven A. Long, *The Teleological Grammar of the Moral Object*
Charles Morerod, OP, *The Church and the Human Quest for Truth*

FUTURE VOLUMES

Kenneth Whitehead, *Vatican II*
Guy Mansini, OSB, *Priesthood*
Edward T. Oakes, SJ, *Jesus Christ*
John Yocum, *The Sacraments*

MAGISTERIUM

∎ ∎ ∎

Teacher and Guardian of the Faith

AVERY CARDINAL DULLES, SJ

Sapientia Press
of Ave Maria University

Requests for permission to make copies of any part of the work should be directed to:

Sapientia Press
of Ave Maria University
1025 Commons Circle
Naples, FL 34119
888-343-8607

Cover Design: Eloise Anagnost

Cover Image: The First Chapter of the 25th Council of Trent, Venetian School, ca. 1630 by Italian School.
© Phillips, The International Fine Art Auctioneers, UK
© Bonhams, London, UK/The Bridgeman Art Library

Printed in the United States of America.

Library of Congress Control Number: 2007920574

ISBN-10: 1-932589-38-4

ISBN-13: 978-1-932589-38-2

TABLE OF CONTENTS

■ ■ ■

APPENDICES

PREFACE

■ ■ ■

IN MY TEACHING CAREER I have often had occasions to give courses on revelation and its transmission in the Church. These courses have included, as a key element, some discussion of the official Magisterium, which is usually exercised in the Catholic Church by the pope and the bishops. In recent years I have experienced difficulty in finding a clear, concise, up-to-date manual on this subject, even though there exists an abundance of literature on different aspects of the teaching office. During the past twenty or thirty years, many important documents have been issued, clarifying points previously disputed. Most students, not to mention members of the general public, are very unclear about the respective authority of various teachers in the Church. Very few understand the different types and degrees of authority attaching to various types of document. Most of the faithful are likewise confused about the biblical sources and the historical development of the Magisterium as a normative organ of doctrinal authority.

For all these reasons I was delighted when Professor Matthew Levering of Ave Maria University asked me to contribute a volume to the series of textbooks being produced by Sapientia Press. I eagerly agreed to produce a short volume on Magisterium. My principal intentions are to explain the rationale for such an organ in the Church, to assess the biblical grounding for its claims, to present a survey of its historical development, and to expound the functioning of the Magisterium in the contemporary Church, including the much-debated question of infallibility. I particularly wanted to include the instructions issued by the Congregation for the Doctrine of the Faith under the supervision of its prefect,

Cardinal Joseph Ratzinger, now Pope Benedict XVI. Any treatment of the Magisterium that overlooks his teaching and that of Pope John Paul II would be in serious need of updating.

In this book I have drawn liberally on my own previous articles on Magisterium, as indicated in the notes and bibliography. In particularly I have followed the main lines of my article on Magisterium for the German *Handbuch der Fundamentaltheologie*, originally published in 1988 and revised for the 2000 edition.

I gladly acknowledge the help of many hands. My assistant, Dr. Anne-Marie Kirmse, OP, has been constantly at my side, making sure that the text and references are clear and accurate. My secretary, Mrs. Maureen Noone, my former graduate assistant, Dr. Jonathan Armstrong, have also provided many services, and Mr. Michael M. Canaris, my present graduate assistant, has helped immensely in the proofreading. Professor Robert Fastiggi of the Sacred Heart Seminary in Detroit and Professor Lawrence J. Welch of the Kenrick-Glennon Seminary in St. Louis have kindly read the manuscript and offered a number of welcome suggestions. Mrs. Diane Eriksen of the Sapientia Press has efficiently seen the manuscript through several critical stages and has patiently borne with all of us as we strove to achieve clear and presentable text.

Avery Cardinal Dulles, SJ
Feast of St. Robert Bellarmine
September 17, 2006

ABBREVIATIONS

■ ■ ■

ABBREVIATIONS USED IN TEXT AND FOOTNOTES

AA   Vatican II, Decree on the Apostolate of the Laity, *Apostolicam actuositatem.*

AAS   *Acta Apostolicae Sedis.* Rome, 1909ff.

ASuc   Directory for the Pastoral Ministry of Bishops, *Apostolorum successores.* Vatican City, 2004.

CD   Vatican II, Decree on the Bishops' Pastoral Office in the Church, *Christus Dominus.*

CDF   Congregation for the Doctrine of the Faith.

CCC   *Catechism of the Catholic Church*

CIC   Codex Iuris Canonici. Vatican City, 1983.

CSEL   *Corpus Scriptorum Ecclesiasticorum Latinorum.* Vienna, 1866ff.

Denz   *Denzinger*

DS   *Enchiridium Symbolorum, Definitionum, et Declarationum,* ed. H. Denzinger, rev. A. Schönmetzer. Freiburg i. Breisgau, 32d ed., 1963.

DV   Vatican II, Dogmatic Constitution on Divine Revelation, *Dei Verbum.*

EJ   National Conference of Catholic Bishops, Pastoral Letter, "Economic Justice for All," 1986.

EV   John Paul II, Encyclical *Evangelium vitae* (The Gospel of Life), 1995.

GS   Vatican II, Pastoral Constitution on the Church in the Modern World, *Gaudium et spes.*

LG   Vatican II, Dogmatic Constitution on the Church, *Lumen gentium.*

Mansi   *Sacrorum Conciliorum nova collectio,* ed. J. D. Mansi, continued by L. Petit and J. Martin, 1759ff.

PG   J. P. Migne, ed., *Patrologiae cursus completus, series graeca.* Paris, 1857ff.

PL   J. P. Migne, ed., *Patrologiae cursus completus, series latina.* Paris, 1844ff.

UR   Vatican II, Decree on Ecumenism, *Unitatis redintegratio.*

UUS   John Paul II, Encyclical on Christian Unity, *Ut unum sint,* 1995.

VS   John Paul II, Encyclical on Certain Fundamental Questions of the Church's Moral Teaching, *Veritatis splendor,* 1993.

CHAPTER ONE

■ ■ ■

The Nature and Function of the Magisterium

THE THREEFOLD OFFICE

ACCORDING TO the Bible and the ancient tradition of the Church, Jesus Christ fulfilled and united in himself the three offices of prophet, priest, and king. As prophet, he succeeded and brought to fulfillment the work of a whole series of prophets from Moses to Elijah, from Jonah to Malachi. As priest, he fulfilled what had been given in type through Melchizedek, Aaron, and the Levites. As king, he was Son of David, the royal Messiah.

Before his Ascension Jesus conferred a share of all these functions on the Church and its leaders. According to the final verses of Matthew's Gospel he commissioned the Eleven to teach, to baptize, and to issue commands. The Apostles and their successors have the power to teach all nations the way of Christ, to sanctify the faithful through sacraments and other forms of worship, and to exercise pastoral government over the community of Christian believers. The Second Vatican Council (1962–65) adopted the threefold division of functions in its Constitution on the Church and in several other key documents.[1]

---

[1] Joseph Lécuyer, "La triple charge de l'évêque," in *L'Église de Vatican II*, ed. Guilherme Baraúna, Unam Sanctam 51c, vol. 3 (Paris: Éd. du Cerf, 1966), 891–914.

The priorities among the three tasks of the hierarchy are mutual. The sanctifying office has priority in the order of final causality, since it is the goal of the others. Governance is primary in the sense that it is a condition of possibility for the exercise of all ecclesial activities. But the prophetic or teaching office holds primacy in the sense that it gives meaning to the other two. As Monsignor Robert Sokolowski has said,

> Teaching is related to sanctifying and governing in a way analogous to the way the theological virtue of faith is related to hope and charity. Faith opens up the whole domain of Christian life; it opens the space in which hope and charity can occur. Likewise, apostolic teaching opens the possibility for Christian life and for the Church. It establishes the space in which sanctification and governance can take their place, and it makes clear what the sanctification and governance really are.[2]

The passing on of revelation pertains specifically to the prophetic office. The Church as a divine oracle is commissioned to bear authoritative witness to God's revelation in Christ. The Greek term *prophētēs*, from which our word "prophet" is derived, means one who speaks for another. In their prophetic role, authorities in the Church speak not in their own name but on behalf of God, whose word they transmit with whatever explanations may be necessary.

The term "Magisterium," the subject of this book, designates the Church's function of teaching.[3] More precisely, it means the

---

[2] Robert Sokolowski, *Christian Faith & Human Understanding* (Washington, DC: The Catholic University of America Press, 2006), 117. Chapter 8 of this book is a paper on "The Identity of the Bishop" presented at a theological conference in 2003.

[3] The standard book in English remains Francis A. Sullivan, *Magisterium: Teaching Authority in the Catholic Church* (New York: Paulist, 1983). The present work grows out of many years of teaching and writing. Its nucleus is Avery Dulles, "Lehramt und Unfehlbarkeit," in the *Handbuch der Fundamentaltheologie*, edited by Walter Kern, Hermann J. Pottmeyer, and Max

authoritative teaching of those who are commissioned to speak to the community in the name of Christ, clarifying the faith that the community professes. The term "Magisterium" designates not only the function of official teaching but also the body of persons who carry on this function, the official teachers. To distinguish it from the less authoritative teaching of individuals in the Church, the word "Magisterium" is sometimes qualified by adjectives such as "hierarchical" or "pastoral."

The offices of teaching, sanctifying, and ruling are closely interrelated in the Church, since all of them are exercised by the same persons with a view to the same end—the salvation of souls. The Magisterium preaches and teaches "holy doctrine" with a view to eliciting the salvific response of faith. Its authoritative teaching imposes a certain obligation on members of the Church to believe. Unlike civil societies, the Church is a society of faith. Its members are united by professing the same body of revealed truth, expressed in creeds and dogmas. To reject the faith of the community is to exclude oneself from the Church as a society. The teaching of the Magisterium therefore has an obligatory force resembling that of a law or precept. But the two are not the same. The ruling power calls for external obedience; the Magisterium calls for free, internal assent. The ruling power speaks first of all to the will; the Magisterium, to the intellect.

In the atmosphere of contemporary liberal democratic societies, the very idea of an authoritative Magisterium provokes misgivings. People tend to think that they have both the right and the duty to make up their own minds about what to believe in matters of religion. They may be willing to take advice from theologians and biblical scholars who have professional qualifications, but they balk at the idea that some body of pastors without specialized academic training should presume to tell them what

Seckler, 1st ed., vol. 4 (Freiburg: Herder, 1988), 153–78; revised for the 2nd ed., vol. 4 (Tübingen: A. Francke, 2000), 109–30.

they must believe. How, they ask, can it be morally justifiable to surrender one's personal responsibility and turn over to others the power of decision in matters of such moment?

THE RATIONALE FOR THE MAGISTERIUM

The Catholic Church believes and teaches that Christ delivered his revelation to the Church as a corporate body. Having received the word of God, the Church has an inalienable responsibility to hand it on, explain it, and defend it against errors. In order to perform this function the Church needs persons and offices with the competence to speak in the name of God. Anyone who wants to ascertain the word of God must obtain it directly or indirectly from the persons to whom it was entrusted. Jesus selected and trained the Twelve for this function. The Bible itself is the work of qualified witnesses who wrote with a special divine assistance known as inspiration. The inspiration of the Old Testament is affirmed in several key passages from the New Testament, most explicitly 2 Timothy 3:14–17 and 2 Peter 1:20–21.

In establishing the Magisterium, Christ responded to a real human need. People cannot discover the contents of revelation by their unaided powers of reason and observation. They have to be told by people who have received it from on high. Even the most qualified scholars who have access to the Bible and the ancient historical sources fall into serious disagreements about matters of belief. Puzzled by the words of Scripture, they feel like the Ethiopian eunuch. When asked by the deacon Philip, "Do you understand what you are reading?" he replied, "How can I, unless someone guides me?" (Acts 8:30–31).

It is logical to suppose that if God deems it important to give a revelation, he will make provision to assure its conservation.[4] If he did not set up reliable organs of transmission, the revelation would

---

[4] John Henry Newman presents the argument under the caption, "An Infallible Developing Authority to Be Expected," chapter 2, section 2, of his

in a few generations be partly forgotten and inextricably commingled with human speculations, as happened, for instance, in Gnosticism. The New Testament and the early Fathers attest that Jesus conferred upon his Apostles and their successors the authority to teach doctrine in his name. As we shall see in chapter II, he promised to remain present with the apostolic leadership to the end of time, and he conferred the Holy Spirit to assist the leadership in remaining faithful. Just as the Christians of the first generation had to rely on the word of the Apostles and their fellow-workers, so the Christians of later generations must continue to rely on the living authority of those who succeed to the place of the Apostles.

THE MAGISTERIUM AND FAITH

The authority of the Magisterium is closely linked with the structure of Christian faith as personal self-surrender to the word of God.[5] Faith is never the mere self-assertion of believers but an acceptance by them of something received from others—in the last analysis, from God. The faithful submit to the word of God as something higher and more reliable than their own personal insights. The word comes through revelation given in history. God's word, moreover, has a content to which the believer must assent. Christianity from its beginnings has been a faith with a definite set of beliefs, expressed in confessional or credal statements.

The propositions of faith are revealed truths; they are not the personal views of a particular theologian or school of theology. Academic theology is not, and does not claim to be, the word of God. Its theses do not merit the absolute assent of faith. Richly blessed though she is by her theologians, the Church needs in

---

Essay on the Development of Christian Doctrine (Notre Dame, IN: University of Notre Dame Press, 1989), 75–92.

5 On the doctrine of faith here presupposed, see Avery Dulles, *The Assurance of Things Hoped For: A Theology of Christian Faith* (New York: Oxford University Press, 1994).

addition an office or organ capable of certifying revealed truth with divine authority. Otherwise she could not serve as "the pillar and bulwark of the truth" (1 Tim 3:15). The Magisterium is an essential resource for theology itself, for without it theology would lack a secure foundation on which to base its speculations. Theology seeks to understand as far as possible the truths that Christians believe as matters of faith.

The acceptance of a faith proclaimed by a divinely commissioned witness is not, as some imagine, an abdication of personal responsibility. It is, on the contrary, a preeminently free and personal act. Freedom is given to us so that we may personally seek and embrace the truth, committing ourselves to live according to it. Since the truth that matters for salvation is offered to us by way of revelation, and since revelation is handed down by competent witnesses, our acceptance of these witnesses is inseparable from the act of faith itself. To withhold assent from the testimony of properly authenticated witnesses to revelation would be a misuse of freedom.

The task of showing that it is reasonable and prudent to submit to the word of God as taught by the Magisterium pertains to apologetics. The present book is primarily doctrinal, not apologetical, in purpose. It is written for believers who adhere to the Christian faith and wish to know more about its authoritative transmission. Principally, this book is for the instruction of Catholics, who have in their Church an active, living Magisterium. One of the tasks of doctrinal theology is to expound in the light of faith the nature and functions of the Magisterium.

THE MAGISTERIUM AND REVELATION

The Magisterium does not have the power to proclaim new revelations, still less to impose its own version of the truth. The popes and councils teach very clearly that the Magisterium is not an original source of revelation, but a witness to a revelation handed down from the past. The Second Vatican Council in its Dogmatic Constitution on Divine Revelation declared that the teaching of the Magisterium "is not above the word of God, but serves it, teaching what has been handed on, listening to it devoutly, guarding it scrupulously, and explaining it faithfully by divine commission and with the help of the Holy Spirit; it draws from the deposit of faith everything that it presents as divinely revealed" (*DV* 10).

Although the nature and sources of revelation are not the subject of this book, something should be said about revelation in relation to the Magisterium.[6] The Catholic Church teaches that the real source of Christian revelation (or the gospel) is Jesus Christ himself. Before the New Testament existed, the Apostles and their associates proclaimed the gospel by word of mouth and by letters, presenting it as the fulfillment of all that had been prophesied and anticipated in the Old Testament. The Council of Trent, in its Decree on the Sacred Scriptures and Apostolic Traditions (1546), declared:

> The gospel was promised of old through the prophets in the Sacred Scriptures. Our Lord Jesus Christ, the Son of God, first promulgated it with his own lips; he in turn ordered it to be preached through the Apostles to all creatures as the source of all saving truth and rule of conduct. (*DS* 1501)

The Second Vatican Council in its Constitution on Divine Revelation addresses this very point once again, using almost the same language as Trent used four centuries earlier (*DV* 7).

THE MAGISTERIUM AND SCRIPTURE

The Apostles and their fellow-workers recognized the Jewish Bible as inspired; the New Testament quotes it in Greek translations,

---

6 René Latourelle, *Theology of Revelation* (Staten Island, NY: Alba House, 1966); Avery Dulles, *Models of Revelation* (New York: Doubleday, 1983; reprinted Maryknoll, NY: Orbis, 1992).

which for the most part agree with the Septuagint version produced in Alexandria. In the course of time certain writings of the Apostles and their close associates came to be read in the churches as authoritative texts, together with passages from the Hebrew Bible. In this way the Church acquired a Bible consisting of two Testaments, the Old and the New.[7]

The Bible, understood in its totality, is a final authority in the sense that it may not be contradicted. But Tradition and the Magisterium are necessary to ensure the correct use and interpretation of Scripture. On the basis of Tradition the Magisterium drew up the canon of Scripture and assumed responsibility for safeguarding the sacred books as an authoritative record of revelation in its constitutive period. By its unceasing vigilance the Magisterium preserves the Scriptures as a sacred deposit and supervises editions, translations, and commentaries. The Council of Trent, in 1546, published a list of the canonical books; it forbade them to be interpreted in opposition to the Church's constant teaching or the unanimous teaching of the Fathers. The Second Vatican Council in its Dogmatic Constitution on Divine Revelation, *Dei Verbum,* devoted four of the six chapters to the authority and use of Holy Scripture. The rule of faith, for Catholics, includes sacred Scripture, sacred Tradition, and the sacred Magisterium. These three elements are so intimately conjoined that they constitute a single composite norm. In the words of Vatican II,

> It is clear, therefore, that sacred Tradition, sacred Scripture, and the Magisterium of the Church, in accordance with God's most wise design, are so linked and joined together that one cannot stand without the others, and that all together and each in its own way under the action of the one Holy Spirit, contribute effectively to the salvation of souls. (*DV* 10)

---

7 Karl Rahner, *Inspiration in the Bible,* rev. trans. (New York: Herder and Herder, 1964).

MAGISTERIUM AND TRADITION

As the preceding quotation indicates, the Magisterium does not function in a vacuum. It is so closely connected with Tradition that the two can never be separated. Indeed, the pronouncements of the Magisterium are one of the forms in which Tradition comes to concrete expression. Holy Scripture is likewise an inspired expression of ancient Jewish and early Christian Tradition, certified to be such by the Church. Other expressions of Tradition may be found in sacred liturgy, in the writings of the Fathers and saintly theologians, and in the collective sense (or "consensus") of the faithful. Confining our attention to the Magisterium, we shall not here deal directly with Scripture or these other forms of Tradition.[8] Magisterial utterances normally come as answers to pressing pastoral problems and must be interpreted in relation to them. Church authorities are often responding to theological proposals, approving or rejecting them as the case may be. The reader of the following chapters should keep this wider context in mind, so as not to isolate the Magisterium unduly from the context in which it operates.

PROSPECTUS

Although it should be clear at this point that the Church does and must have a Magisterium, many problems remain to be investigated. Did the Church in New Testament times already have a functioning Magisterium? After treating this question in chapter 2, we shall inquire into the ways in which the forms of the Magisterium have developed and changed over the centuries (chapter 3). Who in particular are the members of the Magisterium, authorized to speak in the name of Christ the Teacher? If the pope and the bishops constitute the Magisterium, how is their teaching

---

[8] On tradition and the forms of its expression, see Yves Congar, *Tradition and Traditions: An Historical and a Theological Essay* (New York: Macmillan, 1966); *The Meaning of Tradition* (San Francisco: Ignatius, 2004).

authority related to that of saintly Fathers and Doctors of the Church and that of theologians, who teach by reason of their academic proficiency (chapter 4)? Can there be disagreements among different organs of the Magisterium? Does each individual bishop have magisterial authority, or is authority limited to the whole body of bishops? What of particular groups of bishops? Can the pope teach by his own authority, or must he obtain a consensus among his fellow bishops (chapter 5)?

What is the sphere of competence of the pastoral Magisterium? Under what circumstances, if ever, does the Magisterium enjoy infallibility? Are its formulations ever defective and in need of correction or updating (chapter 6)?

What is the obligatory force of magisterial teaching? Does it always call for the assent of faith, or are there lesser degrees of assent that are appropriate for non-revealed truths or noninfallible pronouncements? Is the obligation to assent always absolute and unconditional, or may one give only a qualified assent to certain teachings? Is it ever permissible to dissent (chapter 7)?

The meaning of magisterial decisions, in turn, has to be studied with reference to the way they are understood and interpreted by pastors, theologians, and the faithful. The study of the Magisterium, therefore, would be incomplete without some attention to the process of reception. Reception has played an important role in the ecumenical dialogues of the past century (chapter 8).

CHAPTER TWO

■ ■ ■

The Magisterium
in the New Testament

Jesus as Teacher

ACCORDING TO the biblical vision, all power and wisdom have their origin in God, from whom every good and perfect gift descends (Jas 1:17). Jesus Christ is for Christians the power and wisdom of God (1 Cor 1:24). In him are hidden all the treasures of wisdom and knowledge (Col 2:3). The disciples rightly call him teacher and Lord (Jn 13:13). Jesus tells them that they are not to be called masters, since that title belongs to Christ alone (Mt 23:10).[1] He astonishes his hearers by the authority with which he teaches (Lk 4:32). He does not hesitate to abrogate portions of the Mosaic Law, replacing them with precepts of his own (Mt 5:21–48). Even when he utters "hard sayings," his disciples cling to him as the one who has the words of eternal life (Jn 6:68).

---

[1] Matthew 23:8–12 deals with honorific titles, not with the teaching office. It has to be interpreted in the light of other Matthean passages in which the Lord instructs the disciples to "teach all nations" with his own abiding assistance. See Joseph A. Fitzmyer, "The Office of Teaching in the Christian Church according to the New Testament," in *Teaching Authority and Infallibility in the Church*, ed. Paul C. Empie et al., Lutherans and Catholics in Dialogue 6 (Minneapolis: Augsburg, 1980), 186–212, at 200–202.

Proclaiming a new and astonishing gospel during his earthly ministry, Jesus gathers great crowds who flock to hear his word. But he is not content to preach to anonymous and fickle crowds. He forms a small band of close disciples and trains them rigorously in his doctrine and way of life. The Gospels speak of a group of seventy disciples (Lk 10:1), and within it of a smaller group of twelve, whom Jesus carefully chooses to be Apostles after a night in prayer (Lk 6:12–16). To them he expounds the mysteries of the kingdom of heaven (Mk 4:11). He sends them forth on a mission to announce his message during his public life (Mt 10:5–42), and before his Ascension commissions them to "teach all nations" (Mt 28:18–20).

Even among the Twelve there is a hierarchical order. Jesus selects three of them (Peter, James, and John) to witness the raising of Jairus's daughter, his own glorious Transfiguration, and his Agony in the Garden.

AUTHORITY OF PETER

By all accounts the chief Apostle is Peter, always mentioned first among the Twelve. At Caesarea Philippi (Mt 16:18–19) Jesus designates him as the rock on whom the Church is to be built, gives him the keys of the kingdom of heaven, and empowers him to bind and to loose—terms probably signifying the authority to make binding decisions for the whole community. At the Last Supper he assures Peter: "I have prayed for you that your faith may not fail; and when you have turned again, strengthen your brethren" (Lk 22:32). On Easter Sunday Jesus appears to Peter before the other Apostles (Lk 24:34; cf. 1 Cor 15:5). At the Sea of Tiberias the risen Lord commissions Peter to feed his lambs and his sheep (Jn 21:15–17).

In the early chapters of Acts, we see Peter as the unquestioned leader and spokesman of the apostolic leadership (Acts 1:15; 2:15; 4:8; 5:29; 10:24, etc.). In the two letters ascribed to him we see

Peter from "Babylon" (a code name for Rome) directing his fellow presbyters of other communities. All the texts referring to Peter are pregnant with significance for Catholics, who see the office of Peter continued in the popes.

AUTHORITY OF THE APOSTLES

The term "Apostle" in the narrowest sense refers to the Twelve who were personally called by Jesus and were witnesses to his public life, teaching, death, and resurrection.[2] In his public life Jesus gave them the powers of binding and loosing, previously conferred on Peter alone (Mt 18:18; cf. 16:19). The risen Christ commissioned them (or the Eleven after the defection of Judas) to bear witness to him "to the end of the earth" (Acts 1:8) and promised to be with them "to the close of the age" (Mt 28:20).

Some New Testament texts clearly identify the Apostles with the Twelve (Mt 10:2; Lk 6:13; Rev 22:14) or, after the defection of Judas, with the Eleven (Acts 1:2, 26). But the term "Apostle" is also used more generically to include persons such as Matthias (Acts 1:26), Paul (Rom 1:1; 1 Cor 9:1, 15:8), Paul and Barnabas (Acts 14:4, 14; 1 Cor 9:6). Paul also uses the term less strictly to refer to "messengers of the churches" (2 Cor 8:23) such as Epaphroditus (Phil 2:25). The term is apparently, but not certainly, applied by Paul to James "the brother of the Lord" (Gal 1:19) and to Andronicus and Junias (Rom 16:7).

The New Testament Apostles exercise a variety of functions as witnesses and missionaries. In part their functions are doctrinal, since the faith of the Church is shaped by their testimony. When Paul wants to settle a question doctrinally, he sometimes appeals

---

[2] For an overview of the problem of the apostolic ministry in the New Testament, with bibliography, see Rudolf Schnackenburg, "Apostolicity: the Present Position of Studies," *One in Christ* 6 (1970): 243–73. See also Francis A. Sullivan, *From Apostles to Bishops: The Development of the Episcopacy in the Early Church* (New York: Newman Press, 2001), chapters 1–3.

to his own authority as an Apostle (1 Cor 9:1; 15:9–11; 2 Cor 11:4–6; 12:11–13). For certain formulas of faith he appeals to the unanimous teaching of all the Apostles (1 Cor 15:11) and to the tradition of the earliest Church (1 Cor 11:23; 15:3). Luke, in his idealized portrayal of the primitive Jerusalem community, states that it persevered in the teaching of the Apostles (Acts 2:42)— presumably here meaning the original Eleven together with Matthias as the replacement for Judas.

In the first period the headquarters was the mother church at Jerusalem. Paul went there several times to obtain from Peter and others, who were reputed to be "pillars," official recognition of the gospel he was proclaiming (Gal 1:18–2:10). When a dispute broke out about the need for Christians to observe the Mosaic Law, a consultation was held with the Apostles and presbyters at Jerusalem, who handed down a judgment that they attributed to themselves and the Holy Spirit (Acts 15:1–29).[3]

In general, the founding Apostles seem to have maintained a certain authority over the churches founded by them. Paul and Barnabas (Acts 13:1–3) and later Paul and Sylvanus (Acts 15:40) were commissioned to be the missionary arm of the Antiochene church. Sent out from Antioch, they repeatedly returned to that city to report on their activity and its results.[4]

The original Twelve, together with Matthias and Paul, had the irreplaceable role of being witnesses to the Resurrection and founders of the Church (1 Cor 3:10; Eph 2:20; Rev 21:14). They were conscious of planting the seed that others might water or laying the foundations on which others might build (1 Cor 3:6–7). As witnesses to the saving events, the Apostles preached

---

[3] Avery Dulles, "An Ecclesial Model for Theological Reflection: The Council of Jerusalem," in *Tracing the Spirit: Communities, Social Action, and Theological Reflection*, ed. James E. Hug (New York: Paulist, 1983), 218–41.

[4] Eugene A. LaVerdiere, "The Teaching Authority of the Church: Origins in the Early New Testament Period," *Chicago Studies* 17 (Summer 1978): 172–87, at 183–84.

with full assurance: "Let all the house of Israel therefore know assuredly that God has made him Lord and Christ, this Jesus whom you crucified" (Acts 2:36).

At the headquarters in Jerusalem, it would seem, the Apostles under Peter established the normative formulation of the kerygma and the normative account of the words and deeds of Jesus that underlies the Synoptic Gospels. Paul, though he was not part of the original nucleus, insists that the message he has preached to the Thessalonians is to be accepted not as the word of men but as the word of God (1 Thess 2:13). Since his oral preaching and his letters are of equal authority, the community of Thessalonica is to stand firm and hold to both (2 Thess 2:15). The gospel that he preached to them, Paul declares, came to him not from human sources but from Jesus Christ by way of revelation (Gal 1:12).

As the Apostles of the first generation began to die off, special attention was paid to their letters as monuments to their faith. Leaders of the next generation, it would seem, sometimes exploited the reputation of the founders by attributing to Peter, Paul, James, and John writings composed after their death, turning the founders into literary mouthpieces to give added authority to later works, which were no doubt composed in their spirit and possibly in part dictated by them.[5] The testimony of the apostolic generation is embodied in the Scriptures of the New Testament, which have an abidingly normative character, inasmuch as the Church throughout her history continues to develop in dependence upon her origins, known for what they were. But the New Testament did not simply replace the living apostolic Magisterium. The Church experienced the need for a continuing doctrinal

---

[5] Ibid., 186. On the concept of authorship in the New Testament era, see Raymond E. Brown, "Canonicity," *New Jerome Biblical Commentary*, sec. 89 (Englewood Cliffs, NJ: Prentice Hall, 1990), 1051–52, with references to other literature. Still valuable is the article of Kurt Aland, "The Problem of Anonymity and Pseudonymity in Christian Literature of the First Two Centuries," in the collected work, *The Authorship and Integrity of the New Testament* (London: SPCK, 1965), 1–13.

authority to see to it that the biblical message was faithfully proclaimed and rightly interpreted.

SUCCESSORS OF THE APOSTLES

It is not surprising, therefore, that in certain passages from the Gospels the Apostles are addressed in a manner that would seem to include their successors. For example, in Matthew 28:19–20, Jesus promises to remain present until the end of the age with those whom he sends to speak and act in his name. He instructs these chosen witnesses to make disciples of all nations, to baptize, and to teach. Again, in his high-priestly prayer, Jesus asks the Father to consecrate his disciples in the truth (Jn 17:17–19). In other passages of the Last Discourse the reliability of the Apostles' future testimony is attributed to the Paraclete, the Spirit of Truth, whose assistance is needed for every generation (Jn 14:26, 15:26–27, 16:7–15). Insofar as the Holy Spirit continues to keep the Church in the truth through the testimony of duly commissioned witnesses, the Church perpetually remains apostolic.

Already in the New Testament the Apostles are shown as having the power to commission authoritative ministers of the word and to invoke the power of the Holy Spirit upon them. Paul affirms that no one can preach without being sent (Rom 10:14–18), though he does not here specify who does the sending or how the mission is conferred. Throughout the Book of Acts we find instances of newly commissioned bearers of the faith receiving the required charisms through the laying on of hands. The prophets and teachers at Antioch lay hands on Barnabas and Paul with prayer and fasting when sending them on their first missionary journey (Acts 13:3). Barnabas and Paul take pains to install presbyters in each of the churches they establish in Asia Minor, commending these presbyters to the Lord with prayer and fasting (Acts 14:23). Peter and the Twelve lay hands on representatives of the Greek-speaking Christians at Jerusalem (Acts 6:6). Paul exhorts the presbyter-bishops of Ephesus to carry on his ministry as guardians commissioned by the Holy Spirit (Acts 20:28). To meet a crisis of leadership at Corinth, Paul affirms the authority of Stephanas, Fortunatus, and Achaicus (1 Cor 16:15–18).

The preservation of continuity through duly commissioned, Spirit-guided leaders is further developed in the Pastoral Letters, which give evidence of special concern to safeguard sound doctrine. Paul instructs Titus to appoint in each town of Crete presbyters who can teach with authority, refuting the subverters of orthodoxy (Tit 1:5, 9). He likewise admonishes Timothy, in Ephesus: "What you have heard from me before many witnesses, entrust to faithful men who will be able to teach others also" (2 Tim 2:2). The bishops appointed by Timothy are to be good teachers (1 Tim 3:2). Timothy, having had hands laid on him by the presbyters (1 Tim 4:14) and by Paul (2 Tim 1:6), has received the Spirit of God and is therefore equipped to bear confident witness. Timothy is to lay hands upon others in order that they may do likewise, and is to take care not to lay hands hastily on anyone who may not be properly qualified (1 Tim 5:22). From all these texts it is apparent that the idea of apostolic succession in the ordained ministry is beginning to emerge.

RESPONSIBILITIES OF PASTORS

The Apostles and the bishops and presbyters who gradually entered into their succession received governmental and disciplinary functions as heads of churches. But they also had doctrinal or magisterial responsibilities as preachers and teachers of the faith. Paul in the Second Letter of Timothy says of himself: "For this gospel I was appointed a preacher and apostle and teacher" (2 Tim 1:11). He then reminds Timothy of his duty to "follow the pattern of the sound words" he has heard from Paul and to "guard the truth that has been entrusted to you by the Holy Spirit" (2 Tim 1:13–14). To Titus he writes that a bishop "must hold firm to the sure word as taught, so that he may be able to give instruction in sound doctrine and also to confute those who contradict it" (Tit 1:9).

On occasion Paul and other pastoral leaders go far beyond elementary instruction in the basics of the faith. Paul chides the Corinthians for not being prepared to receive advanced instruction (1 Cor 3:1–2); the author of Hebrews likewise deplores the spiritual immaturity of his readers, who still "need milk, not solid food" (Heb 5:11–14). In Romans Paul presents a highly involved discussion of the doctrine of justification. The author of Hebrews gives a lengthy disquisition on the priesthood of Christ. Although treatises such as these go far beyond the basic Christian kerygma, they are presented as authoritative. The New Testament therefore contains not only elementary proclamation but relatively advanced doctrine pertaining to the faith.

Among the responsibilities of the pastors was the refutation of heresy. Paul in Galatians vehemently attacks the Judaizers who are seeking to require even Gentile Christians keep the Mosaic law. In Colossians he reproves a kind of early Gnostic syncretism that would subordinate Jesus to certain heavenly powers. In his farewell speech at Ephesus Paul exhorts the pastors to be on guard against false teachers who will speak perverse things to draw away the disciples after them (Eph 20:30). In a passage dealing with responsibilities of ministers of the word, Paul warns against those who allow themselves to be tossed about by "every wind of doctrine, by the cunning of men, by their craftiness in deceitful wiles" (Eph 4:14). In the Pauline Pastoral Letters Timothy and Titus are admonished to protect the flock against godless heretics, who teach strange doctrines, myths, and endless genealogies (1 Tim 1:3–4; Tit 3:9). Some, such as Hymenaeus and Philetus, "have swerved from the truth by holding that the resurrection is past already" (2 Tim 2:18).

This concern with orthodoxy is not peculiarly Pauline. Peter in his Second Letter predicts that false teachers will arise and "secretly bring in destructive heresies" (2 Pet 2:1). The Second Letter of John admonishes the community to "abide in the doctrine of Christ" and not even to greet those who fail to adhere to this holy doctrine (2 Jn 9–11). In the Book of Revelation the author warns against the heresy of the Nicolaitans that was infecting some of the Christians at Ephesus and Pergamon (Rev 2:6, 15). Thus the struggle against heresy was even in the first century a major preoccupation of the apostolic Magisterium.

EMERGENCE OF THE EPISCOPATE

The New Testament does not single out any particular office as the bearer of the apostolic succession. Timothy and Titus, although they carry on the ministry of Paul, are not called bishops or presbyters. The bishops *(episkopoi)* of New Testament times, unlike the Apostles, seem to be merely local officers. In some churches (for example, Ephesus as described in Acts) bishops and presbyters *(presbyteroi)* seem to be the same persons under different names (Acts 20:17, 28). Other communities seem to have had either bishops (like Philippi) or presbyters (like Jerusalem) but not both. The grammatically plural use of the word "bishop" *(episkopos)* in Acts 20:28 and Philippians 1:1 seems to indicate that in the early period a single local church could have a plurality of bishops, but the singular use of the same term in 1 Timothy 3:2 and Titus 1:7 may indicate that by the time the Pastoral Letters were composed, the "monarchical" episcopate was emerging. If the "angels" of the seven churches of Asia Minor in the first three chapters of the Book of Revelation are, as many believe, bishops, we have here a confirmation that by late New Testament times each local church in Asia Minor may have had a single bishop as its pastor.

Among the functions of bishops, that of preserving the faith against heretics comes to the fore in certain passages of Acts and especially in the Pastoral Letters. Yet bishops are still under the supervision of Apostles such as Paul and of "apostolic delegates" such as Timothy and Titus. In the Church of subsequent generations the bishops as an order will have succeeded to the order of Apostles. Assisted by the risen Christ and his Spirit, they will have the fullness of doctrinal authority in the post-apostolic Church. The New Testament exhibits Church order in its formative stages, but more time was needed for Church order to assume its definitive form.

CHAPTER THREE

■ ■ ■

The Magisterium:
Historical Development

INDIVIDUAL BISHOPS

CONCERN FOR orthodoxy, which was on the rise in the later New Testament writings, remained intense among the early Fathers.[1] As a remedy against heresy they looked to the teaching of the bishops, who had received the faith as handed down from the Apostles. In the early Christian centuries each local church was headed by a bishop, who was not only the leader but, above all, the teacher of the community. "It was he who initiated the catechumens into the divine mysteries, who fed the faithful with the bread of the word, who formed the clergy and virgins, and who had ultimate responsibility for orthodoxy."[2]

---

[1] On the Magisterium in the patristic age, see John E. Lynch, "Apostolic Fathers to Gregorian Reform," in *Chicago Studies* 17 (1978): 186–209; Robert B. Eno, "Some Elements in the Pre-History of Papal Infallibility," *The Teaching Office and Infallibility in the Church*, ed. Paul C. Empie, 238–58; Damien van den Eynde, *Les Normes de l'Enseignement chrétien dans la littérature patristique des trois premiers siècles* (Paris: Gabalda, 1933).

[2] Basil Studer, "The Situation of the Church," in *A History of Theology*, vol. 1: *Patristic Period*, ed. Angelo Di Berardino and B. Studer (Collegeville, MN: Liturgical Press, 1996), 253–63, at 254.

Near the end of the first century, Clement of Rome lays down the principle, "Christ from God, and the Apostles from Christ" (Clement, *First Epistle to the Corinthians* §42.2; PG 1:292). He adds that the Apostles established bishops and made provision so that when they died other approved men *(viri probati)* would succeed to their ministry (Clement, *First Epistle to the Corinthians* §44.2; PG 1:296).

Ignatius of Antioch holds that just as Christ expresses the mind of the Father, so the bishops express the mind of Christ (Ignatius, *Letter to the Ephesians* §3:2; PG 5:648). He urges the Philadelphians: "Hold aloof from disunion and misguided teaching and, where your bishop is, there follow him like sheep" (Ignatius, *Letter to the Philadelphians* §2.1; PG 5:820). The bishop, who normally teaches in consultation with his presbyters (Ignatius, *Letter to the Trallians* §7.2; PG 5:681), is especially attuned to Christ and gifted to discern heretical deviations from the faith (Ignatius, *Letter to the Philippians* §1.2; PG 5:820).

Irenaeus, toward the end of the second century, develops the theme of apostolic succession in his great work against Gnosticism, *Adversus haereses.* He relates how his own teacher, Bishop Polycarp of Smyrna, faithfully handed down the sacred body of doctrine he had learned from the Apostle John (*Adv. haer.* 3:3:4; PG 7:851–52). The true doctrine of the Apostles, he asserts, comes down through the succession of bishops (*Adv. haer.* 4:33:8; PG 7:1077).

In a phrase not easy to interpret, Irenaeus affirms that the bishops of the apostolic churches, upon their accession to the episcopate, have received the "sure gift of truth" *(charisma veritatis certum)* according to the Father's good pleasure (*Adv. haer.* 4:26:2; PG 7:1053–54). He seems to mean that the bishops are reliable teachers not only because they have received the sacred deposit of faith but especially because the Holy Spirit, through a sacramentally conferred charism, assists them to discern the truth of revelation.[3] In speaking of the *charisma veritatis certum* Irenaeus coins a term that will become standard in future centuries.

Tertullian, about A.D. 200, is convinced that the apostolic churches received their first bishops from the Apostles or from "apostolic men," deriving authority from them. He challenges heretics to prove the apostolic origin of their own traditions (*On Prescription against Heretics* §32; PL 2:44).

Hippolytus, a few years later, affirms confidently that the bishops are successors *(diadochoi)* of the Apostles *(Philosophumena.* 1, proem. 6; PG 16:3020). In the ordination ritual of St. Hippolytus *(Apostolic Tradition,* early third century) the Holy Spirit is invoked upon the bishop that he may "feed the flock"—a traditional New Testament expression for pastoral care with an emphasis on right teaching (cf. Acts 20:28).

Cyprian, in the mid-third century, actually identifies the bishops with Apostles *(apostolos, id est, episcopos—*Ep. 3:3; *CSEL* 2:471).

COUNCILS

Even before the Christianization of the Empire the bishops met frequently in local or provincial synods to settle questions of faith and morals. Although presbyters, deacons, and laypersons were in attendance at such synods, the decision was rendered by the bishops.

As examples one may refer to the third-century synods of Carthage and Rome, at which the Novatian heresy was condemned. About the same time several councils were called in the East to deal with Paul of Samosata, the heretical bishop of Antioch. In the early fourth century an important synod was held at Elvira in Spain to settle disputed questions about marriage, clerical celibacy, baptism, and confirmation. In 314 a Synod of Arles in Southern

---

[3] On the interpretation of this term one may consult Yves Congar, *L'Église une, sainte, catholique et apostolique,* Mysterium Salutis 15 (Paris: Cerf, 1970), 210–11; also Jerome D. Quinn, "Charisma veritatis certum," *Theological Studies* 39 (1978): 520–25.

France prohibited the rebaptism of persons validly baptized in heretical communities, thereby condemning a Donatist practice.

After the conversion of the Emperor Constantine, ecumenical councils began to be held. Since the ecumenical councils of the patristic era were all held in the East, very few Latin bishops actually took part. Nevertheless these councils included, in principle, representative bishops from the whole Christian world. The pope was not personally present, but usually sent delegates, who were treated with great deference. It eventually became a rule that the decisions of the council could not be valid without Roman approval.

The first four ecumenical councils (Nicaea, 325; Constantinople, 381; Ephesus, 431; and Chalcedon, 351) have been recognized as especially important for establishing the Trinitarian and Christological faith of the Church. Going beyond the letter of Scripture, they forged creeds and dogmas that all Christians were obliged to accept. The original four councils together with the next three (Constantinople II, 553; Constantinople III, 680–81; and Nicaea II, 787) continue to be recognized in most major Christian traditions (for example, Orthodox, Catholic, Anglican, Lutheran, and Reformed) as binding, or at least as expressing a right understanding of the revelation entrusted to the Apostles and attested by Holy Scripture.

Many patristic writers, influenced by Acts 15:28, maintain that bishops in council are specially guided by the Spirit.[4] Thus Cyprian, referring to the decisions of a synod at Carthage, writes: "It has pleased us, prompted by the Holy Spirit. . . ." (Ep. 54; PL 3:887). Similar phrases recur in the Acts of the Council of Arles (Mansi 2:469) and in the writings of the Emperor Constantine about the Council of Nicaea, notably his letter to the Church of Alexandria (PL 8:509A). Later Cyril of Alexandria will hold that the Holy Spirit spoke through the Fathers at Nicaea (PG 77:16B).

---

[4] Heinrich Bacht, "Sind die Lehrentscheidungen der ökumenischen Konzilien göttlich inspiriert?" *Catholica* 13 (1959): 128–39.

Leo I likewise teaches that the canons of Nicaea were drawn up "by instruction of the Holy Spirit" (Letter 104 to Emperor Marcian, ch. 3; PL 54:995A). Elsewhere he makes the same claim for the Council of Chalcedon (Letter 144 to Bishop Julian; PL 54:1113A).

Augustine and Vincent of Lerins, in the early fifth century, derive the authority of ecumenical councils primarily from the fact that they express the consensus of the universal Church. Augustine is more disposed than Vincent to admit what we would call development of doctrine. "Who does not know," he asks, ". . . that the regional and provincial councils are entirely subjected to the more plenary councils in which the whole Christian world comes together? that often the earlier plenary councils are corrected by later ones; when, to wit, in virtue of a certain experience of things, gates are opened that before were shut and hidden things come to be known?"[5] Vincent of Lerins was more reluctant to admit change and development. In a famous passage he lays down the canon: *"quod ubique, quod semper, quod ab omnibus creditum est."*[6] For him universality, antiquity, and consensus are the touchstones of truth. But he does admit that the Church's understanding of dogma advances over the years: "Therefore, let there be growth and abundant progress in understanding, knowledge, and wisdom, in each and all, in individuals and in the whole Church, at all times and in the succession of the ages, but only in its proper kind, i.e., in the same dogma, the same meaning, the same understanding."[7]

Whether a given council is ecumenical has not always been evident from the beginning. Constantinople I was a purely Eastern council without any representatives from the West and was not originally envisioned as ecumenical, but it came to be so recognized

---

[5] Augustine, *De Baptismo,* Bk. II, chap. 3; quoted in Jan Walgrave, *Unfolding Revelation* (Philadelphia: Westminster, 1972), 86.

[6] "What has been believed everywhere, always, and by all," Vincent of Lerins, *Commonitorium Primum* 2 (PL 50:640).

[7] Vincent of Lerins, *Commonitorium Primum* 23 (PL 50:668); quoted by Vatican I, *Dei Filius* (*DS* 3020).

when its creed was approved by Chalcedon and accepted in the West as well as the East. Some synods, though convoked as ecumenical, were rejected because they were partisan or even unorthodox: for example, those of Sardica (343), Rimini (359), and Ephesus (449). The adherence of the five great patriarchates (Rome, Alexandria, Antioch, Constantinople, and Jerusalem) was considered important, but in the event of disputes among the other patriarchates, the judgment of Rome prevailed. The Nestorian party at Antioch and the Monophysite party at Alexandria were defeated in the fifth century largely through the influence of Rome.[8]

THE SEE OF ROME

The exercise of Roman primacy over the universal Church developed gradually but steadily from the beginnings, chiefly on the ground that Rome was the city where the most glorious Apostles, Peter and Paul, had ministered and been martyred. Already at the end of the first century Clement, writing in the name of the Church of Rome, admonishes the Corinthian Christians to restore order in their church, where certain properly appointed and blameless pastors had been deposed. Ignatius of Antioch, in his *Letter to the Romans,* salutes the Church of Rome with deep respect: "You are a credit to God; you deserve your renown and are to be congratulated. You deserve praise and success and are privileged to be without blemish. Yes, you rank first in love." (Ignatius, *Letter to the Romans,* proem.; PG 5:685). He confesses that he cannot speak to their church with the authority that Peter and Paul had exercised (Ignatius, *Letter to the Romans* §4.3; PG 5:689).

Irenaeus and others look on Peter and Paul as the founders of the Roman Church, which for that reason enjoys preeminence *(potentior principalitas)* over all the other churches (*Adv. haer.* 3.3.2; PG

---

[8] John Henry Newman in his *Essay on the Development of Christian Doctrine* gives a dramatic description of the decisive role played by Pope Leo I in thwarting the Monophysite heresy. See chapter VI, sec. 3.

7:848). Cyprian, writing to Pope Cornelius in 252, refers to the see of Rome as "the throne of Peter, . . . the chief church, from which the unity of the episcopate has arisen" ("ecclesiam principalem unde unitas sacerdotalis exorta est"; Ep. 59:14; *CSEL* 3.2.683). Pope St. Stephen, a contemporary of Cyprian, claims to speak as successor of Peter in settling the question of the validity of heretical baptisms.

The claim to Petrine primacy will be further developed by a series of popes including Damasus I (366–84), Siricius (384–99), and Innocent I (402–17). Leo I (440–61) perfected the doctrine, claiming that the popes have *plenitudo potestatis* over the universal Church.

In his struggle against Pelagianism Augustine wrote: "For already [the acts of] two councils on this question have been sent to the Apostolic See; and rescripts have also come from there. The cause is finished: would that the error might sometime be finished also!" (Sermon 131; PL 38:734). Prosper of Aquitaine, the talented secretary of Leo I, wrote concerning the Pelagian controversy: "For a right profession of faith in the area of teaching on grace, we regard as sufficient the writings of the Apostolic See. Those who oppose the teachings set forth in them have separated themselves from the Catholic faith."[9]

The Roman claim to primacy was increasingly recognized in the East as well as in the West.[10] The Council of Sardica (modern Sophia, 343–44) recognized Rome as the ultimate court of appeal in disputed cases. Eastern Fathers such as Theodoret of Cyrrhus, Maximus the Confessor, and Theodore the Studite spoke unambiguously of the pope as successor of Peter. The bishops at the Council of Ephesus cheered when the letter of Pope Celestine

---

9 Quoted by Basil Studer, "The Bible as Read in the Church," in Di Berardino and Studer, *History of Theology* 1:353–73, at 373.

10 On the recognition of papal primacy by the Eastern Fathers, see Olivier Clément, *You Are Peter: An Orthodox Theologian Reflects on the Exercise of Peter's Primacy* (Hyde Park, NY: New City Press, 2003), 34–35. The quotations in the present paragraph are from this source.

affirming that Mary is the Mother of God *(theotokos)* was read at the Council. In a Synodal Letter the Council of Chalcedon (451) wrote to Leo the Great: "You came to us; you have been for everyone the interpreter of the voice of Blessed Peter. . . . We were some 520 bishops whom you guided as the head guides the members" (cf. *DS* 306). The sixth ecumenical council (Constantinople III, 680–81) wrote to Pope Agatho: "We place ourselves in your hands, you who occupy the first see of the universal Church, you who rest on the firm rock of faith."

BISHOPS AND THEOLOGIANS IN THE MIDDLE AGES

Throughout the Middle Ages the bishops were considered to be the chief preachers and guardians of the faith. Many of them were also theologians and canon lawyers, and thus there was in practice no gulf between scholarship and the power of office. The relationship between the *clavis scientiae* (the key of knowledge) and the *clavis potestatis* (the key of power) was a subject of much learned speculation. By the thirteenth century it was generally agreed that when the pope uses his power to make a determination of faith, his judgment prevails over the wisdom of scholars.[11]

In the early Middle Ages, continuing well into the twelfth century, local councils, presided over by bishops and papal legates, were heavily involved in judging cases of alleged heresy. Councils of this type considered charges against theologians such as Gottschalk on predestination, Berengarius on the presence of Christ in the Eucharist, Abelard on faith and reason, Gilbert de la Porrée on the Trinity, and many others. Rome, as the last court of

---

[11] Yves Congar has traced the debate about these two "keys" from Maximus of Turin (d. 465) through St. Bede, Anselm of Laon, Abelard, and Gratian. See his "Theologians and the Magisterium in the West: from the Gregorian Reform to the Council of Trent," *Chicago Studies* 17 (1978): 210–24, at 214–15.

appeal, was regarded as the final judge of orthodoxy. The statement, "Whoever does not agree with the church of Rome should not be considered a Catholic," which appears as the twenty-sixth of twenty-seven propositions in the *Dictatus Papae* of Gregory VII, expressed a commonplace.

The popes of the Middle Ages summoned a variety of councils, some of which appear on official lists of ecumenical councils, even though they were exclusively Western. Among the general councils of the West are the four Lateran Councils (1123, 1139, 1179, 1215) and the two Councils of Lyons (1245, 1274).

From the middle of the twelfth century, under strong popes such as Alexander III, Innocent III, and Gregory IX, the prestige of the papacy steadily increased, supported by the new mendicant orders of the thirteenth century. Saints Bonaventure and Thomas Aquinas were among the champions of papal power in the universal Church.

With the rise of the universities, theology professors developed a doctrinal magisterium of their own, which frequently worked in collaboration with the pastoral magisterium of the hierarchy. Papal censures often did no more than ratify lists of condemned propositions prepared by theologians. The University of Paris was considered especially authoritative in its doctrinal determinations.

In the Middle Ages local church councils were often convened not only by ecclesiastics, as stated above, but also by secular rulers to deal with problems arising in society; the decrees of such councils were sometimes reissued as laws of the state. But the general councils convoked by the popes were the preserve of ecclesiastics. Beginning with Lateran IV (1215) certain lay rulers were invited, but were not given a vote.[12] Many non-bishops, including theologians and canonists, took part in various capacities. The doctrinal decrees of several general councils (Lyons I, 1245; Lyons II, 1274;

---

[12] Walter Ullmann, *Medieval Foundations of Renaissance Humanism* (Ithaca, NY: Cornell University Press, 1977), 23, 54–55.

and Vienne, 1312) were submitted to university faculties for approval before being published.[13]

With the Avignon Captivity (1309–77) and the Great Schism (1378–1415) the prestige of the papacy underwent a decline. At the Council of Constance (1415–18), Pierre d'Ailly, former chancellor of the University of Paris, successfully contended that the doctors of sacred theology should have a deliberative vote since they had received the authority to preach and teach everywhere— an authority that "greatly exceeds that of an individual bishop or an ignorant abbot or titular."[14] In its later sessions Constance sought to make the papacy accountable to the Church in council as the locus of supreme power.

In the course of the fifteenth century, however, the balance of power shifted back again from the councils to the popes. The Council of Florence, in its Decree for the Greeks (1439), defined the universal primacy of the Roman pontiff as successor of Peter, Vicar of Christ, head of the Church, and father and teacher of all Christians (*DS* 1307).

The Council of Trent (1545–63) was a modern-style papal-episcopal council, with theologians present in an essentially advisory capacity. While the theologians did not make doctrinal decisions, they were able to exercise a significant influence by debating the decrees in the presence of the bishops before the decrees were promulgated. Taking up the language of Clement and Irenaeus, Trent taught that the bishops have succeeded to the place of the Apostles (*DS* 1768) and decreed, under anathema, that bishops are superior to priests (*DS* 1777). Trent used its authority to define, among other things, the list of canonical books of Scripture (*DS* 1504) and the obligatory force of the Church's interpretation of Scripture (*DS*

---

[13] Cf. Yves Congar, *Vraie et fausse Réforme dans l'Église*, 2d rev. ed., Unam Sanctam 72 (Paris: Cerf, 1969), 461.

[14] The treatise of Cardinal d'Ailly is quoted at some length from Mansi 27:561 by Hans Küng in *Structures of the Church* (New York: Nelson, 1964), 88.

1507). The decrees of Trent on Scripture, Tradition, justification, the sacraments, Purgatory, and indulgences were a point-by-point response to the questions raised by the Protestant Reformers.

FROM TRENT THROUGH VATICAN I

The three or four centuries after Trent witnessed bitter struggles against Gallicanism and Jansenism. Gallicanism was a French movement arising from medieval conciliarism in combination with modern nationalism. Following a declaration by the Sorbonne issued in 1663, the French clergy adopted in 1682 the famous "Four Articles," the fourth of which declared that although the pope enjoys the principal role in questions of faith, his judgments are not irreformable unless and until they are confirmed by the consensus of the Church, that is, the bishops (cf. *DS* 2284). The Gallican Four Articles were repudiated by the Holy See but remained influential for some time in French seminaries.

Jansenism takes its name from the Dutch bishop and theologian Cornelius Jansen (1585–1638), whose massive tome *Augustinus* was posthumously published in 1640. When five propositions from this work were condemned by Pope Innocent X in 1653, many Jansenists refused to submit and embraced Gallicanist positions in ecclesiology. Analogous to Gallicanism in France were movements such as Josephism in Austria and Febronianism in Germany. The Holy See repeatedly condemned lists of Gallican and Jansenist propositions.

In the mid-nineteenth century, a group of German-speaking university professors under the leadership of Ignaz von Döllinger sought a maximum of academic freedom for themselves and minimized the binding force of the official Magisterium. In reply Pius IX reminded Catholic scholars that they are bound not only by the solemn definitions of the Magisterium but also by the ordinary and universal teaching of the whole Church dispersed throughout the world (*DS* 2879).

These centrifugal movements were offset in nineteenth-century Catholicism by papalist movements, known as "Ultramontane." Rejecting ecclesiological nationalism, many devout believers rallied to the support of Rome, thus preparing the way for the vigorous pontificate of Pope Pius IX and for the First Vatican Council.

Pius IX (1846–78) showed great energy in supervising matters of doctrine. After consulting the worldwide episcopate, he in 1854 solemnly defined the dogma of the Immaculate Conception of the Blessed Virgin Mary, thus laying claim implicitly to the power to speak infallibly. In 1864, he issued a famous *Syllabus of Errors* summarizing many of his previous condemnations of current views on faith and reason, pantheism, and religious liberalism. He later summoned the First Vatican Council with the aim of quashing the remains of Gallicanism.

Vatican Council I (1869–70), in its Dogmatic Constitution *Dei Filius,* defined the necessity of accepting on a motive of "divine and Catholic faith" the dogmatic teaching of the ordinary and universal Magisterium of the bishops as well as their solemn teaching when gathered in council (*DS* 3011). In its Constitution on the Church, *Pastor aeternus,* Vatican I defined the pope's primacy of jurisdiction and his infallibility (*DS* 3064, 3074). The Lord, it taught, had endowed Peter and his successors with the "charism of unfailing truth and faith," so that the whole flock of Christ might be protected from the poison of error, be nourished with the food of heavenly doctrine, and as a result stand firm against the powers of hell (*DS* 3071). Although Vatican I did not have time to give full consideration to the episcopal office, it declared that bishops were appointed by the Holy Spirit (cf. Acts 20:28) and succeeded to the place of the Apostles (*DS* 3061). It envisaged a cooperative relationship between the pope and the bishops, who governed their respective dioceses as true pastors (ibid.).

In 1875 the German bishops, responding to Chancellor Otto von Bismarck, explained that Vatican I had not substituted the pope's authority for that of the bishops, but had left their pastoral authority intact (*DS* 3112–16). Pope Pius IX approved of this interpretation of the Council. John Henry Newman and other commentators on Vatican I gave a balanced interpretation that effectively answered the charges that the Council had turned the Church into an absolute monarchy, making the bishops mere delegates of the pope.[15]

The Modernist crisis at the dawn of the twentieth century raised questions about the relations between faith and history. Because the Modernists sought to obtain complete freedom for scholars to exercise their critical reason in accordance with contemporary scientific methods, the Magisterium took the occasion to reassert the authority of popes and bishops to impose permanently binding dogmatic decisions. The Oath against Modernism (1910) contained the words: "I hold with equally firm faith that the Church, the guardian and teacher of the revealed word, was proximately and directly instituted by the true historical Christ himself during his life among us, and that it is built on Peter, the head of the apostolic hierarchy and upon his successors through the ages" (*DS* 3540).

During the 1940s a movement of return to the biblical and patristic sources, sometimes called "ressourcement" or "la nouvelle théologie," aroused some misgivings in Scholastic circles. Pius XII in his Encyclical *Humani generis* (1950) reminded scholars that the Magisterium is the proximate and universal norm of revealed truth (*DS* 3884) and that the pope has authority to terminate debate on disputed issues without recourse to his supreme power in an ex cathedra pronouncement (*DS* 3885). In this way he reinforced what is called the ordinary teaching power of the pope.

Pius XII (1939–58) issued important encyclicals on the study of Scripture, the Church, and the liturgy. In 1950 he invoked his

---

15 John Henry Newman, *Letter to the Duke of Norfolk,* chs. 8 and 9, and Conclusion; reprinted in Alvan Ryan, ed., *Newman and Gladstone: The Vatican Decrees* (Notre Dame, IN: University of Notre Dame Press, 1962), 167–203.

ex cathedra power to define the Assumption of the Blessed Virgin Mary, proceeding the same way as Pius IX, when he defined the dogma of the Immaculate Conception. The pontificate of Pius XII in many ways prepared for the Second Vatican Council (1962–65), which reaffirmed many of his teachings, while placing them in a broader conception of the Magisterium. In the remainder of this book, we shall deal with contemporary Catholic teaching, which is most authoritatively set forth by Vatican II. In the next chapter, we shall consider who speaks for the Church in matters of faith, and in subsequent chapters, we shall address the additional questions mentioned above at the end of chapter 1.

CHAPTER FOUR

■ ■ ■

Hierarchical and Nonhierarchical Teachers

IN MODERN Catholic teaching the term "Magisterium" generally designates the hierarchical teachers—the pope and the bishops—who by virtue of their office have authority to teach publicly in the name of Christ and to judge officially what belongs to Christian faith and what is excluded by it. This concept of the Magisterium, though it seems almost self-evident today, is relatively recent. Before the nineteenth century, the dichotomy between private and public, unofficial and official, was not so clearly drawn.

HISTORICAL DEVELOPMENT

In the first millennium, according to Max Seckler, there was a kind of "perichoresis," or mutual interpenetration, between Magisterium and theology.[1] The bishops held office as pastors in the apostolic succession, and in that capacity were responsible for heralding the faith and protecting it against attacks. But in so doing the bishops themselves reflected on the faith and sought to understand what

---

[1] Max Seckler, "Kirchliches Lehramt und theologische Wissenschaft, geschichtliche Aspekte, Probleme und Lösungselemente," in *Die Theologie und das Lehramt*, ed. Walter Kern (Freiburg: Herder, 1982), 17–62, at 21–26.

they believed. The great teachers of sacred doctrine were for the most part bishops, though there were notable exceptions such as Tertullian, Clement of Alexandria, Origen, Ephrem, and Jerome. These non-bishops engaged not only in theological speculation but also in the proclamation and defense of the faith, and sometimes played a prominent role in the formulation of official doctrine. For example, Athanasius, while still a deacon, participated actively in the debates at the Council of Nicaea.

With the rise of the universities in the high Middle Ages a clearer division of labor emerged. The *studium* (academy), having its center in Paris, came to be recognized as a third locus of authority, alongside the *sacerdotium* (priesthood in the sense of spiritual authority), centered in Rome, and the *imperium* (secular rule), situated at the capital of the Empire. So esteemed were these three hierarchical authorities that they were sometimes compared to the three persons of the Trinity, with the Holy Spirit corresponding to the *studium*.[2] The *studium* had its primary seat in the universities, in which persons with suitable academic qualifications were appointed to professorial chairs by competent ecclesiastical authority. Such professors were *magistri* or *doctores* (masters, doctors); they exercised what Thomas Aquinas, for example, called a *"magisterium cathedrae magistralis"* (a magisterium of the professorial chair). The bishops, by contrast, had a "magisterium cathedrae pastoralis" (a magisterium of the pastoral chair). Aquinas linked the pastoral magisterium with *praelatio*, or governing power in the Church.[3] The magisterium of the theologians consisted in scholarly research and teaching.

---

[2] Walter Ullmann, *Medieval Foundations of Renaissance Humanism* (Ithaca, NY: Cornell University Press, 1977), 76–77.

[3] Yves Congar, "A Brief History of the Forms of the Magisterium and Its Relations with Scholars," in *The Magisterium and Morality*, Readings in Moral Theology No. 3, ed. Charles E. Curran and Richard A. McCormick (New York: Paulist, 1982), 314–31. On p. 314 the terminology of St. Thomas is summarized, with references to his writings. See also Seckler, "Kirchliches Lehramt," 32.

In chapter 3 we have seen how the university theology faculties took on certain official responsibilities in the Church of the late Middle Ages. Universities such as those of Louvain and Cologne played a major part in drawing up the list of propositions from Luther's writings that were condemned by Pope Leo X in his bull *Exsurge Domine* (1520). A generation later, the faculties of Louvain and Paris, together with Alcalá and Salamanca, drew up lists of censurable propositions found in the writings of Baius (Michel de Bay). Francisco de Vitoria (ca. 1485–1546) went so far as to affirm that it would be a mortal sin to approve of a contract that had been judged usurious by the University of Paris.[4] Catholic universities continued to claim a certain magisterial authority until most of them were suppressed after the French Revolution.

Although the theory of St. Thomas on the twofold Magisterium is unexceptionable, the concept of the scholarly magisterium was subject to abuse. In the centuries after his death the university faculties exerted considerable power over the hierarchy itself, prevailing on bishops to condemn positions disapproved by the professors. As a result the hierarchical magisterium became heavily involved in academic questions, some of them quite intricate. Popes and bishops for some time frowned on the admission of Aristotle into the university curriculum. Some of the medieval doctrinal condemnations are phrased in technical terms that seemed to favor particular philosophical systems and schools. But the vigilance of the pastors over the academy did keep heresy at bay in academically turbulent times. The neo-Scholastic textbooks of the nineteenth and early twentieth centuries retained St. Thomas's twofold conception of magisterium. Ioachim Salaverri, for example, recognizes both a *magisterium docens,* which uses human argumentation, and a *magisterium attestans,* which bears authoritative witness to the deposit of

---

4 Yves Congar, "Theologians and the Magisterium in the West: From the Gregorian Reform to the Council of Trent," *Chicago Studies* 17 (1978): 210–24, at 220.

faith.[5] Francis A. Sullivan, in the 1965 edition of his manual on ecclesiology, makes a similar distinction.[6] According to this schematization, theologians as well as bishops have a true magisterium, but not a parallel or competing one.

The modern concept of the Magisterium as an exercise of hierarchical authority is connected with the threefold division of powers discussed above in chapter 1. This schematization came into favor early in the nineteenth century, when canon lawyers applied to the Church ideas that secular political theorists had formed with reference to the sovereign state.[7] Just as certain government officials were empowered to speak and act for the state, so, the canonists reasoned, the Church must have certain officials competent to speak and act for her as a society. They were public persons, capable of performing acts attributable to the Church as such. Just as the state had legislative, judicial, and administrative powers, so the Church had powers to teach, sanctify, and rule. In this framework it became common to speak not only of *a* magisterium but of "*the* Magisterium," with the definite article and an upper-case M.

---

[5] Ioachim Salaverri, *De Ecclesia Christi,* no. 503, in *Sacrae Theologiae Summa,* vol. 1: *Theologia Fundamentalis,* 3d ed. (Madrid: Biblioteca de Autores Cristianos, 1955), Part III, no. 503, 662–63.

[6] Francis A. Sullivan distinguishes between *magisterium mere docens, seu scientificum,* and *magisterium attestans,* which can obligate the hearer to assent in faith, because of the divine mission of the teacher. See his *De Ecclesia,* vol. 1, 2d ed. (Rome: Gregorian University, 1965), 258–59.

[7] The threefold division of powers, including the Magisterium alongside of the powers to rule and sanctify, was promoted by the German canonist Ferdinand Walter in his *Lehrbuch des Kirchenrechts* (1829) and by the Austrian canonist Georg Phillips in his seven-volume *Kirchenrecht* (1845–72). Josef Fuchs in his dissertation *Magisterium, Ministerium, Regimen. Vom Ursprung einer ekklesiologischen Trilogie* (Bonn, 1941) has traced the rise of this schematization in Catholic theology. Yves Congar published a French translation of this dissertation in a bulletin for the *Revue des sciences philosophiques et théologiques* 53 (1969): 185–211. For a more general survey of the development of the theory of powers in the Church, see Giuseppe Alberigo, *Lo Sviluppo della dottrina dei poteri nella Chiesa universale* (Rome: Herder, 1964).

If we take the term "Magisterium" in this modern sense, it has to be understood as a function of the hierarchy, that is to say, the pope and the bishops, who succeed to Peter and the Apostles in teaching and pastoral rule. As we shall see in future chapters, there are many different modes of exercise of hierarchical teaching authority. Sometimes it is exercised by the whole body of bishops together with the pope as its head; sometimes by the pope alone; sometimes by individual bishops or groups of bishops. The exercise, moreover, can be more or less formal and solemn, resulting in different degrees of obligation on the part of the faithful to assent.

Once the term "Magisterium" is understood in its modern, narrow sense, as the power to teach officially in the name of Christ and to issue judgments binding on the faith of others, it becomes evident that theologians do not, as such, have a magisterial status. Their specific task is to penetrate and explain the meaning, grounds, and implications of Christian faith. Although they strive to be of service in the Church, they are not mere servants of the hierarchy. Their primary responsibility is to discern and interpret the word of God by all the means available. In this role they are expected to do more than echo what the Magisterium has already taught, but they have no authority to oblige others to accept their conclusions.

PARTICIPATION IN THE HIERARCHICAL MAGISTERIUM

According to the modern use of the term "Magisterium," the pope and the bishops alone must be said to possess public teaching responsibility by virtue of their office. But they may at their discretion associate others with themselves. Non-bishops have at times exercised a variety of magisterial functions. In the first few centuries Christian emperors were considered competent to convoke councils, preside over them (though without a vote), and promulgate their decrees. The Church of that time does not seem to have objected.

In the Middle Ages secular princes, religious superiors, and theologians frequently took part in ecclesiastical councils. Under the provisions of the 1917 Code of Canon Law, the list of those who have a right to attend ecumenical councils with deliberative vote included not only bishops but all cardinals (even those who were not bishops), certain abbots, the superiors general of exempt clerical religious orders, and others (canon 223). In the revised Code of 1983 non-bishops are still eligible to be invited to ecumenical councils with deliberative vote (canon 339). In such cases they are temporarily aggregated to the Magisterium.

Ecclesiastical councils, moreover, are only one example of the non-hierarchical exercise of the Magisterium. Vatican II, in its Decree on the Pastoral Office of Bishops, stated that even pastors who are not bishops are charged with a teaching function (*munus magisterii*; *CD* 30). Since they have this responsibility by reason of their office, they are recognized as participants in the Church's Magisterium, not in the sense of being able to define new doctrine or impose censures on dissident Catholics, but in the sense of being responsible to instruct their parishioners in the faith.

The same may be said, in varying degrees, of all who teach Christian doctrine by reason of an official mandate or *missio canonica*. Seminary professors and members of ecclesiastical faculties are commissioned to transmit not their personal insights but rather the faith of the Church.[8] Catechists are expected not to inculcate their private opinions but to hand on the Christian message and insert it more deeply into the minds and hearts of their students.[9] The participation of theologians in the public teaching of the Church often takes place by way of consultation. Because scholarship is respected

---

[8] According to the Apostolic Constitution *Sapientia christiana* (1975), a canonical mission is necessary because teachers of sacred disciplines in ecclesiastical faculties "do not teach on their own authority, but by virtue of a mission they have received from the Church." General Norms, Article 27 §1.

[9] John Paul II, Apostolic Exhortation *Catechesi tradendae*, 5, 20, and passim.

as a path to truth, it is customary for popes and bishops to consult experts in fields such as Scripture, Church history, theology, and canon law before issuing their doctrinal pronouncements. Conciliar documents and encyclicals are not uncommonly drafted by theologians under the direction of hierarchical teachers.

Vatican II, in its Constitution on Divine Revelation, states that while Scripture scholars, through their preparatory study, help to mature the judgment of the Church, the interpretation of Scripture is finally subject to the judgment of the Church, meaning the hierarchical Magisterium (*DV* 12). The same may be said analogously of the scholarly work of theologians. They make proposals but do not establish Catholic doctrine. "The task of authentically interpreting the word of God, whether written or handed down [in Tradition], has been trusted exclusively to the living Magisterium of the Church" (*DV* 10).

After the Magisterium has spoken, theologians play an indispensable role in giving effect to its pronouncements. Just as they took part in preparing the way for the pronouncements to be made, so too they inform the public about what has been decreed and in so doing interpret the documents. Every papal or conciliar definition or condemnation leaves a certain margin for interpretation, so that private judgment has to complete what public pronouncements left unstated. John Henry Newman insisted on this point in his defense of the Vatican decrees on papal primacy and infallibility. Once a thesis or treatise is censured, he writes, "theologians employ themselves in determining what precisely it is that is condemned in that thesis or treatise; and doubtless in most cases they do so with success, but that determination is not *de fide*."[10] Newman considers this process of theological sifting a necessary safeguard, protecting the faithful against the "fierce and intolerant temper" of those who would brush aside theological

---

[10] Newman, "Letter to the Duke of Norfolk," Ryan, *Newman and Gladstone*, 193.

distinctions and burden the consciences of the faithful with exorbitant demands.[11]

THE CONSENSUS OF THEOLOGIANS

The standard textbooks of neo-Scholastic theology recognize the convergence of distinguished theologians of different schools in favor of, or in opposition to, certain doctrines as evidence that the former doctrines are in accord with the faith while the latter are not. Theologians, they recognize, are not simply scholars seeking to understand the faith; they are also witnesses to the faith that they seek to interpret. The scholarly opinions of theologians do not carry the same authority as their testimony to the faith; they are only as valid as the supporting arguments they adduce. As mentioned above, some neo-Scholastic textbooks make a distinction between the "attesting magisterium" of the bishops and the "scientific magisterium" of theologians. This terminology, while it can be defended, gives a false impression. Theologians, we must recall, are not scientifically detached professors of religious studies. Like bishops, they are committed believers. They do not proceed always and only by syllogistic argumentation, but make ample use of the "sense of the faith" that the Holy Spirit infuses into the hearts of believers. The finest theologians are not only brilliant dialecticians; they are also Christians who pray, worship, and strive to live the faith. Their theology, as a consequence, indirectly attests to their faith.[12] Theologians, therefore, can exercise an "attesting magisterium" of sorts.

In his classic work on the sources of theology, *De locis theologicis*, Melchior Cano drew up a very influential list of ten theological loci. In this list the consensus of Fathers and concordant teaching of theologians rank immediately after ecumenical councils and papal deter-

---

[11] Ibid., 197.

[12] Hans Urs von Balthasar, "Theology and Sanctity," in his *Word and Redemption*. Essays in Theology 2 (Montreal: Palm, 1965), 49–86.

minations.[13] Regarding the Fathers, Cano contends, as did St. Thomas before him, that their witness as individuals gives probability but no more. By exception, individual Fathers can err, but, according to Cano, it is impossible for all the Fathers to err in matters of faith.[14] As for the Scholastic theologians, it would be close to heresy *(haeresi proximum)*, he states, to contradict their unanimous opinion on a matter of faith and morals.[15]

FATHERS AND DOCTORS OF THE CHURCH

As indicated by the preceding citation from Melchior Cano, the Fathers of the Church hold a preeminent place among theological authorities. Already in the sixth century, the Gelasian Decree "On Books to Be Received and Not Received" lists on the positive side, immediately after Holy Scripture and the acts of the ecumenical councils, the writings of the Fathers that are accepted in the Catholic Church. The authors here listed include not only the great bishop-doctors of the East and West but also the presbyter Jerome and the layman Prosper of Aquitaine (*DS* 353). The Council of Trent, a millennium later, forbids anyone to interpret the Scriptures against the consensus of the Fathers (*DS* 1507)—a prohibition that was to be repeated by the First Vatican Council (*DS* 3007) and several biblical encyclicals. In holding that the unanimous consent of the Fathers on doctrines of faith is infallible, Melchior Cano is by no means singular. He represents the common opinion of Scholastic theologians, confirmed by the magisterial statements to which I have alluded.

Although many of the Fathers were bishops, the Fathers are not identical with the Magisterium. Their role is a distinct one:

---

[13] Melchior Cano, *De locis theologicis,* 1st ed., 1562; reprinted in *Theologiae cursus completus,* vol. 1 (Paris: J. P. Migne, 1839), cols. 58–715. Book VII deals with the authority of the Holy Fathers; Book VIII, with the authority of the Scholastic doctors.

[14] Ibid., Bk. VII, chap. 3, cols. 368–89.

[15] Ibid., Bk. VIII, chap. 4, col. 400–403.

that of writers of Christian antiquity who have received recognition from later centuries as being eminent for orthodoxy and holiness. Since their recognition comes more from Tradition than from any specific act of the Magisterium, no official list of Church Fathers exists. Any credible list, however, would have to include those traditionally recognized as the four great doctors of the East (Athanasius, John Chrysostom, Basil the Great, and Gregory Nazianzen) and the four great doctors of the West (Ambrose, Augustine, Jerome, and Gregory the Great).[16]

The term "doctor" has various meanings in various contexts. Originally it referred to the more eminent Fathers, but as a Scholastic title it was unofficially applied to a vast number of medieval and early modern theologians. St. Augustine, for instance, is called the *doctor gratiae*, Thomas Aquinas the *doctor angelicus*, and Francisco Suárez the *doctor eximius* (the exceptional doctor).

The official title "Doctor of the Church" has been bestowed on certain canonized saints who have been singled out by popes or councils for their eminence in learning and soundness of doctrine. Doctors in this sense do not have to be members of the Magisterium. Nearly half of the thirty-three were not bishops. A few, such as St. Ephrem, were never ordained to the priesthood. Under Paul VI and John Paul II three women were added to the catalogue of doctors: Catherine of Siena, Teresa of Avila, and Thérèse of Lisieux.

The "Sense of the Faithful"

Besides the specially gifted persons discussed in the preceding pages, all Christians have, through faith and baptism, a "sense of the faith," which is generally more acute in proportion to their personal faith and holiness. The Spirit-filled community is a

---

[16] On the authority of the Fathers, see Congar, *Tradition and Traditions,* 435–50, and idem, *The Meaning of Tradition,* 143–50; Joseph Ratzinger, "Importance of the Fathers for the Structure of Faith," in his *Principles of Catholic Theology* (San Francisco: Ignatius, 1987), 133–52.

bearer of revelation, and its experience of the faith is an authentic theological font. The hierarchy, as Cardinal Newman pointed out, frequently consults the laity before defining doctrines.[17] After a doctrine is proclaimed, the laity are obliged to accept it, loyally deferring to the Magisterium (*LG* 12). The consensus of the faithful, including both the ordained and the laity, is an infallible sign of truth, provided that they universally agree that the doctrine in question is a matter of faith (*LG* 12). The assent of the faithful, when it is spontaneous and joyful, gives a desirable reinforcement to the teaching of the pastors. As Vatican II insisted, every Christian is expected to be a witness to the faith and to that extent a teacher (*LG* 10, 33; *AA* 6, and so on). But the teaching function of ordinary laypersons is not normally called a magisterium, for it is neither hierarchical nor academic.

The sense of the faithful should be carefully distinguished from public opinion in the Church, which is not a theological source attributable to the Holy Spirit, but a merely sociological fact. Public opinion may be correct, but it often reflects the tendencies of our fallen human nature, the trends of the times, and the pressures of the public media.

It frequently happens that prophets and mystics, without being either bishops or theologians, make statements touching on doctrine. It is probable that, as saintly persons, they may have privileged insights into the designs of God or the implications of the faith. They can give striking expression to aspects of the gospel but do not exercise a magisterium of either a personal or an academic nature. The value of their judgments is to be appraised by the community of faith (1 Thess 5:19–21) and the pastors (Vatican II, *LG* 12). Unless approved by ecclesiastical authorities, purported private revelations should be treated with prudent reserve. On all accounts, they should not be confused with articles of faith.

---

[17] John Henry Newman, *On Consulting the Faithful in Matters of Doctrine* (Kansas City, MO: Sheed and Ward, 1985).

As a result of the survey in this chapter we may conclude that Christian doctrine is transmitted by a great variety of witnesses, who have different kinds and degrees of authority. Theologians who work in communion with the Church may be said to exercise a magisterium distinct from, but related to, that of the hierarchy. They may on occasion be called to participate in the official teaching of the hierarchy. The official Magisterium, however, belongs by right to the pope and his fellow bishops. They alone have the divinely given responsibility to teach with the authority of Christ and to formulate doctrine for the Church as such. They exercise what is called, in a special sense, *the* Magisterium.

CHAPTER FIVE

■ ■ ■

Organs of the Magisterium

THE MAGISTERIUM, in current Catholic usage, consists of the pope and the bishops who are in hierarchical communion with him. They can teach in a variety of ways, but do so most solemnly when they perform a joint action for which all are co-responsible. But it is also possible for the pope to teach alone as visible head of the pilgrim Church and for individual bishops or groups of bishops to speak on questions of doctrine. Different organs of the Magisterium speak with different degrees of authority.

THE COLLEGE OF BISHOPS

The doctrine that bishops who are in communion with Rome constitute a college has deep roots in patristic theology, notably in the work of Cyprian.[1] After some centuries of neglect, the doctrine was further obscured in the late Middle Ages and the Counter-Reformation, when Catholic theologians were seeking to defend papal authority against the attacks of Conciliarists, Protestants, and Gallicans. Some theologians so exalted the authority of the pope that they made the bishops appear to have no authority

---

[1] Jean Colson, *L'Épiscopat catholique: collégialité et primauté dans les trois premiers siècles de l'Église* (Paris: Cerf, 1963).

except that which he delegated to them. But the idea of collegiality reemerged toward the end of the eighteenth century.[2] At the dawn of the nineteenth century, Gregory XVI, in a work published before he became pope, approvingly quoted Vincenzo Bolgeni to the following effect: "Each bishop in the act and by force of his ordination begins to be a member of the episcopal body *(corpo episcopale)* and as a result receives the right to govern and administer the whole Church whenever he is in union with all the others and constitutes a body with them."[3]

Vatican I in *Dei Filius* recognized the binding authority of the ordinary and universal Magisterium (*DS* 3011) and in *Pastor aeternus* affirmed the unity of the episcopate under the successor of Peter as its principle of unity (*DS* 3051). Had time permitted, the Council would probably have adopted a draft decree on the episcopate that upheld collegiality.

Along the same line of progression, Pope Pius XII in his encyclical on missionary activity, *Fidei donum* (1957), attributed responsibility for the apostolic mission of the Church conjointly to the whole body of bishops. "If each bishop is the sacred shepherd of that part only of his flock which has been entrusted to him, nevertheless inasmuch as by divine ordinance and precept he is a legitimate successor of the Apostles, together with the rest of the bishops he becomes responsible for the apostolic task of the Church."[4]

Vatican II, in *Lumen gentium,* made the doctrine of collegiality the linchpin of its theology of the episcopate. The episcopal order

---

[2] See the discussion of E. D. Cristianopoulo, G. V. Bolgeni, P. Ballerini, and F. A. Zaccaria in Yves Congar, *L'Église de S. Augustin à l'époque moderne* (Paris: Cerf, 1970), 402–5.

[3] Mauro Cappellari (Gregory XVI), *Il trionfo della Santa Sede e della Chiesa* (Venice: Giuseppe Ballaggia, 1832), 119. The text is quoted by J. Robert Dionne in his *The Papacy and the Church: A Study of Praxis and Reception in Ecumenical Perspective* (New York: Philosophical Library, 1987), 388–89.

[4] Pius XII, Encyclical *Fidei donum*; text in *AAS* 49 (1957): 225–48, at 237. See Dionne, *Papacy and Church,* 64–65, 389–90.

as a whole, together with the successor of Peter as its head, succeeds to the college of the Apostles in possessing full and supreme power in the universal Church (*LG* 22). Each bishop receives with ordination the three functions *(munera)* discussed above in chapter 1: those of sanctifying, teaching, and governing. The capacity to exercise the *munus* of sanctifying, as occurs in sacramental actions such as the consecration of the Eucharist, is inseparable from the order itself, and can never be lost. The *munera* of teaching and pastoral rule, however, cannot be exercised except by bishops in hierarchical communion with the head and members of the episcopal college (*LG* 22). Hierarchical communion, a condition for the exercise of these latter functions, is ruptured by schism or heresy.

Bishops, as understood by Vatican II, are men who have received by episcopal consecration the fullness of the sacrament of order.[5] Some bishops receive a canonical mission to govern a diocese, but even without such a mission they are bishops in the full sense of the word.[6] According to canon law, every bishop in good standing is a member of the episcopal college and, as such, is co-responsible for the total mission of the Church. Each such bishop is entitled to participate in ecumenical councils (CIC, c. 336, 339).

Ecumenical councils are gatherings of bishops from the whole world. The pope, and he alone, has the prerogative of convoking and presiding over such councils. Their decrees, to be valid, must be confirmed or at least approved by him (*LG* 22). This view of councils is a development beyond the ancient view, in which the Emperor normally convoked councils and gave juridical force to their decrees; it differs also from the medieval conciliarist theory, in which the bishops could decide, independently of the pope, when and how often they would meet in council. The teaching of Vatican

---

[5] See John Paul II, Apostolic Exhortation *Pastores gregis* (2003), §8.

[6] John Paul II in *Pastores gregis* declared: "Precisely because the College of Bishops is a reality prior to the office of heading a particular Church, there are many Bishops who, while carrying out tasks that are properly episcopal, are not heads of particular Churches" (§8).

II on ecumenical councils, unlike the imperialist and conciliarist models, reflects a correct theology of primacy and episcopacy.

At ecumenical councils the bishop-members are present not simply as consultors but as true pastors and judges of the faith. The decrees of such councils emanate conjointly from the pope and the other members. The formula of promulgation adopted at Vatican II was composed with great care to indicate the primatial role of the pope and the collaboration of the other bishops. The formula, at the conclusion of each document, reads as follows:

> Each and every one of the things set forth in this Constitution [or Decree or Declaration] has won the consent of the Fathers of this most sacred Council. We, too, by the apostolic authority conferred on us by Christ, join with the Venerable Fathers in approving, decreeing, and establishing these things in the Holy Spirit, and we direct that what has thus been enacted in synod be published to God's glory.

Paul VI signed first with the title "Bishop of the Catholic Church." Then followed the signatures of the other Fathers.

While promoting collegiality, Vatican II in no way limited the plenitude of power attributed to the pope by previous councils. It reaffirmed the teaching of Vatican I on papal primacy and infallibility. Like that council, *Lumen gentium* referred to the standard Petrine texts from the Gospels as biblical support. "Our Lord," it stated, "made Simon Peter also the rock and key-bearer of the Church (cf. Mt 16:18–19) and appointed him shepherd of the whole flock (cf. Jn 21:15ff)" (*LG* 22). The Roman pontiff, moreover, is the supreme teacher of the faithful and has the charge of confirming his fellow bishops in the faith (*LG* 25; cf. Lk 22:32).

Lumen gentium also repeats the assertion of *Pastor aeternus* that the pope's doctrinal definitions have validity "by themselves, not by reason of the consent of the Church" *(ex sese, non autem ex consensu Ecclesiae*; *DS* 3074; cf. *LG* 25). Vatican II interpreted this statement as meaning that the pope's definitive decrees, protected by the promised assistance of the Holy Spirit, "need no approval from others, nor do they allow an appeal to any other judgment." Then, borrowing from what Bishop Vinzenz Ferrer Gasser had said as reporter for the Deputation on Faith at Vatican I,[7] *Lumen gentium* added that when the Magisterium teaches definitively, "the assent of the Church can never be wanting, on account of the activity of that same Holy Spirit, whereby the whole flock of Christ is preserved and progresses in unity of faith" (*LG* 25).

Some interpreters of collegiality have contended that the pope could never define matters of doctrine by his own authority, without obtaining the consent of the body of bishops. *Lumen gentium,* however, declared that the pope can always exercise his supreme power freely (*LG* 22). The Doctrinal Commission gave further clarifications in its "Prefatory Note of Explanation," which is considered authoritative for the right interpretation of chapter III of *Lumen gentium,* since Paul VI directed that it be attached to the conciliar text. This note asserts that the pope as Vicar of Christ and visible head of the entire Church has powers that are unique to himself. He can decide whether to act separately *(seorsim)* or together with the other bishops, as the welfare of the Church may seem to require. The college, moreover, cannot perform strictly collegial acts, such as defining doctrine, except when it is called into action by its head.

---

[7] Bishop Gasser stated in his official *Relatio* of July 11, 1870: "Finally, we do not separate the Pope, even minimally, from the consent of the Church, as long as that consent is not laid down as a condition which is either antecedent or consequent. . . . Indeed, since we believe that the Pope is infallible through the divine assistance, by that very fact we also believe that the assent of the Church will not be lacking to his definitions since it is not able to happen that the body of bishops be separated from its head, and since the Church universal is not able to fail." See J. D. Mansi, *Sacorum Conciliorum Nova Collectio,* vol. 52, 1204–30, at 1214; English translation of Gasser's *Relatio* in James T. O'Connor, ed., *The Gift of Infallibility* (Boston: St. Paul Editions, 1986), 44.

One might ask whether it is coherent to maintain that there are two supreme subjects of power in the same institution, namely, the pope and the college of bishops. The majority of theologians reply that since these two subjects are inadequately distinct, there is no problem. The college always includes the pope as its head. He can act alone or conjointly with the whole college, but the college cannot act without him. If the other bishops tried to act in opposition to him, he could abstain from approving their action, thereby rendering it invalid. He has the choice of speaking either *with* the bishops as primate of the college or *to* the whole Church (including the bishops) as supreme Vicar of Christ.[8]

THE POPE AS HEAD

All agree that the pope as head is able to perform certain acts that other members of the college cannot perform. One school of theologians, who sometimes point to Matthew 16:19 and 18:18, contend that the Lord made Peter his vicar and head of the Church before he formed the apostolic college and endowed it with similar powers. Hence it follows that the pope's powers are independent of those belonging to the college of bishops. Theologians of another school contend that the pope is head of the Church and Vicar of Christ only because, and insofar as, he is head of the college of bishops. Karl Rahner, for example, contends that the pope never exercises his supreme power except in his capacity as head of the episcopal college. He writes: "To 'act alone' [in the sense of the Prefatory Note of Explanation] only excludes the necessity of a strictly collegiate act of the bishops, but not the fact that he acts precisely as head of the college when he

---

[8] For an excellent presentation of the theological opinions of the relations between primacy and collegiality, see Yves Congar, *Ministères et communion ecclésiale* (Paris: Cerf, 1971), 187–227.

decides 'alone'."[9] Neither opinion is ruled out by the documents of Vatican II.

At Vatican II the popes withheld from the Council certain questions such as birth regulation, which in their judgment could be better handled without the publicity and social pressures of a conciliar debate. Since Vatican II, as previously, the popes have made important doctrinal pronouncements, not indeed without consultation but without summoning the entire episcopate to collegial action. In future chapters we shall touch on the doctrinal weight of several types of papal pronouncement.[10]

DICASTERIES OF THE HOLY SEE

Besides teaching in his own name, the pope may teach through dicasteries of the Roman Curia: the Secretariat of State, the congregations, tribunals, councils, offices, and commissions. The prefects and members of the congregations are cardinals and bishops. Appointed by the pope, they serve at his pleasure as a kind of cabinet. The acts of congregations, though not issued in the name of the pope himself, gain juridical authority by being approved by him either in a general way *(in forma communi)* or specifically (in *forma specifica*). In the latter case they are equivalently acts of the pope himself. Official teachings of the Holy See normally come into force after publication in the *Acta Apostolicae Sedis* (CIC, c. 8).

Among the dicasteries, the Congregation for the Doctrine of the Faith (CDF) has special importance for promoting and safeguarding sound doctrine in the sphere of faith and morals. In its promotional function, it sponsors studies and research for a better understanding of the faith and for dealing with new problems. In

---

[9] Karl Rahner "Dogmatic Constitution on the Church, chapter 3, arts. 18–27," in *Commentary on the Documents of Vatican II*, vol. 1, ed. H. Vorgrimler (New York: Herder and Herder, 1967), 186–218, at 204.

[10] In chapters 6 and 7 mention will be made of Paul VI, *Humanae vitae,* and John Paul II, *Ordinatio sacerdotalis* and *Evangelium vitae.*

its protective function, it calls attention to deviations from orthodoxy and warns the faithful against them. The CDF is also charged
with the task of formulating the required Profession of Faith.[11] The
prefect of the CDF is ex officio president of the Pontifical Biblical
Commission and the International Theological Commission. Both
these commissions are advisory to the Holy See.[12]

The Pontifical Biblical Commission enjoyed a high degree of
authority when first established by Leo XIII in 1902 and especially under Pius X, who confirmed its authority by an apostolic
letter of 1907. But many of its responses to questions asked in the
early part of the century were time-conditioned prudential directives to Catholic teachers and writers rather than strictly doctrinal
pronouncements requiring internal assent. Since Paul VI's reform
of the Roman Curia in 1971, the Biblical Commission is no
longer an organ of the Magisterium but a trusted group of scholars appointed by the Holy See.

BISHOPS IN GROUPS

Official Church teaching can emanate not only from universal
organs (the college of bishops, the pope, and dicasteries of the Holy
See) but also from groups of bishops and individual bishops. Particular groups of bishops cannot perform strictly collegial acts, since
the college is indivisible: By definition it includes the entire body of
bishops who are in communion with the successor of Peter. Groups
of bishops are nevertheless urged to operate in a collegial spirit. In
the language of Vatican II, they possess *affective* collegiality (*colle-
gialis affectus, LG* 23); but this should not be misunderstood as
implying that they cannot be *effective* in significant ways.

The Synod of Bishops is one of the principal organs of collegiality. Consisting as it does of a relatively small number of bishops

---

[11] John Paul II, Apostolic Constitution *Pastor bonus* (1988), nos. 48–54.
[12] Ibid., 55.

meeting for a restricted time, it cannot perform strictly collegial acts, but it can greatly assist the pope in his exercise of solicitude for the entire Church. The pope could on occasion empower an assembly of the Synod to issue a binding doctrinal or legislative pronouncement, but thus far he has not done so. The reports issuing from assemblies of the Synod deserve to be received with respect, especially because they have been approved by the pope before being promulgated. Frequently the pope summarizes the results of these assemblies by writing Post-Synodal Apostolic Exhortations that enjoy his personal authority. The exact ecclesial status of the Synod of Bishops is still in flux and is debated among experts.[13]

In the first millennium particular councils were of great doctrinal importance. Because communications were slow and difficult, many questions had to be settled locally before being referred to the Holy See or to the full body of bishops. In chapter 3 mention has been made of ancient councils such as those of Carthage, Sardica, Orange, and Toledo. In the Middle Ages important councils were held in Quiercy, Frankfurt, Soissons, Rheims, and elsewhere, dealing with the doctrines of the Trinity, predestination, the real presence, and other important questions. Although particular councils lack authority to speak to the universal body of the faithful, their decrees have sometimes gained general acceptance by being confirmed through the approval of popes and ecumenical councils or, less formally, through the general consensus of bishops and theologians.

In modern times, with the increase of doctrinal activity on the part of the Holy See, particular councils no longer have the same

---

13 Jozef Tomko, ed., *Sinodo dei Vescovi: Natura, Metodo, Prospettive* (Vatican City: Libreria Editrice Vaticana, 1985); François Dupré la Tour, *Le Synode des Évêques et la Collégialité* (Malesherbes, France: Parole et Silence, 2004). For a brief discussion in English, see Avery Dulles, "Synod of Bishops," in *The New Dictionary of Catholic Social Thought*, ed. Judith A. Dwyer (Collegeville, MN: Liturgical Press, 1994), 930–32.

doctrinal importance. In the United States the three plenary councils of Baltimore (1852–84) were important for many practical issues, but not for their doctrinal decisions. Since Vatican II there have been very few plenary or national councils, and provincial councils have likewise become infrequent. As envisaged by current canon law, particular councils must include not only bishops but a selection of clergy, religious, and lay faithful (CIC, c. 443). The Code states that such councils exercise the "power of governance," and make provision "for the pastoral needs of the people of God," but it says nothing of their teaching authority (c. 445). In any case, their decrees cannot be promulgated until they have been reviewed by the Holy See (c. 446). They therefore have no independent teaching authority.

Since Vatican II episcopal conferences have practically taken the place of plenary councils. As explained by Vatican II and the Code of Canon Law (*CD* 38; CIC, c. 447), they are intended primarily as organs for consultation, so that the bishops of the region may coordinate their policies.

Whatever "magisterium" the conferences possess is pastoral rather than strictly doctrinal. To meet the needs of their own nation or region, they call attention to certain teachings of the universal Church and apply them to the local situation. In the United States, the National Conference of Catholic Bishops issued a number of collective pastoral letters, most importantly "The Challenge of Peace" (1983) and "Economic Justice for All" (1986). These pastorals contained some social doctrine, but the bishops explained that they were only seeking to apply what was already the universal teaching of the Church. In the letter on the economy they asserted that their applications were "prudential judgments" that did not have the same authority as doctrinal declarations (EJ 20).

The theological status and teaching authority of episcopal conferences were clarified by Pope John Paul II in his motu proprio *Apostolos suos* of May 21, 1998. This was followed in 2004 by the

Directory for the Pastoral Ministry of Bishops, *Apostolorum succes-sores*. According to these documents episcopal conferences have, among other functions, that of transmitting the doctrine of the Church in ways suited to the particular character and circumstances of life of the faithful of the region (*ASuc* 28).

Under certain circumstances established by law (CIC, c. 455 §2) episcopal conferences may issue doctrinal decrees, but in such cases their statements must be approved unanimously by the bishop members or else by a two-thirds majority of the bishops with deliberative vote. In the latter case, the Holy See must grant recognition before the decrees take effect (*ASuc* 31). These restrictions are in order because the plenary power of the Magisterium resides only in the whole apostolic college and its head. Episcopal conferences, since they lack the fully collegial character of the whole body of bishops, cannot bind their member bishops in matters of doctrine.

INDIVIDUAL BISHOPS

Following in the footsteps of previous councils, Vatican II asserted that individual bishops are successors of the Apostles (*LG* 18) and that this succession has taken place by divine institution (*LG* 20). Although they are not infallible as individuals, all bishops are authoritative teachers, possessing what Irenaeus described as "the sure charism of truth" (*DV* 8). Their charism, however, does not operate automatically. They must, like Timothy, "rekindle" the gift of God that is in them through the laying on of hands in the apostolic succession (cf. 1 Tim 1:6). Bishops are encouraged to take time for personal study and to consult well-qualified theological advisers.

Residential or diocesan bishops, according to Vatican II, are authentic teachers, charged especially with the preaching of the gospel, a task they perform in the name of Christ (*LG* 25). The diocesan bishop is expected to teach, and to do so in communion with the college of bishops and with the successor of Peter. His should be, so to speak, "the voice of the local church in which the universal Church is rendered present in a particular place."[14] As the moderator of the ministry of the word for his diocese, the bishop must see to it that the word of God is rightly preached and taught in the diocese by priests, deacons, and religious educators. He has primary responsibility for catechesis in the diocese.

For an adequate understanding of the Magisterium it is important to recognize the identity and variety of its bearers, as the present chapter has sought to do. But more remains to be done. We must consider the areas in which the various organs are competent and the degrees of authority with which they may choose to speak. In some areas, we shall see, the pope and the college of bishops, assisted by the charism of infallibility, are able to teach definitively in the name of Christ.

---

[14] National Conference of Catholic Bishops, "The Teaching Ministry of the Diocesan Bishop: A Pastoral Reflection," *Origins* 21 (January 2, 1992): 473–92, at 480. See also John Paul II, Apostolic Exhortation *Pastores gregis*, chapter 3, and Directory for the Pastoral Ministry of Bishops, *Apostolorum successores*, chapter 5, "The *Munus Docendi* of the Diocesan Bishop."

CHAPTER SIX

■ ■ ■

The Scope of the Magisterium: Infallibility

THE TEACHING MISSION of the Magisterium does not extend to everything knowable. The Church does not herself teach mathematics, medicine, or economics, though she might have things to say about some of these subjects from her own perspective. Vatican II summarizes in one compact sentence the functions of the official Magisterium. It states that the bishops "preach to the people committed to them the faith they must believe and put into practice. By the light of the Holy Spirit, they make that faith clear, bringing forth from the treasury of revelation new things and old (cf. Mt 13:52), making faith bear fruit and vigilantly warding off any errors that threaten their flock (cf. 2 Tim 4:14)" (*LG* 25).

THE TREASURY OF REVELATION

The Magisterium as here described draws its teaching from revelation. The "treasury of revelation" may be taken as a synonym for the more common term "deposit of faith," which occurs in the Pastoral Letters (1 Tim 6:20; 2 Tim 1:12, 14). The terms "treasury" and "deposit" are metaphors for the gospel, that is, the divine revelation that culminated in the Christ-event. As many theologians have observed, one should avoid objectifying the "deposit" as though it consisted simply of divinely given propositions rather than the concrete, living reality to which the Apostles bore witness (cf. 1 Jn 1:12).[1]

Vatican II's Dogmatic Constitution on Divine Revelation teaches that the fullness of revelation was given in the incarnate life, death, and glorification of the Son of God and in the sending of the Spirit of Truth. "No further public revelation is to be awaited *(expectanda est)* before the glorious manifestation of our Lord Jesus Christ" (*DV* 4). It is no doubt possible to identify revelation with God's continual self-communication as this occurs through nature, through historical events, and through the proclamation of the gospel. Even so, however, it must be granted that nothing is revealed that is not in some way contained in Jesus Christ, who is the "mediator and at the same time the fullness of all revelation" and who was revealed once and for all to the Apostles (*DV* 2; 7–8).

Christians of every century share one and the same faith, that "which was once for all delivered to the saints" (Jude 3). They do so, however, as people of their own time, accepting the faith as interpreted by the living Church to which they belong.

FUNCTIONS OF THE MAGISTERIUM

The first function of the Magisterium is that of heralding the apostolic faith. In order to preach the gospel effectively it is not enough to repeat verbally what is stated in Scripture and in the documents of Tradition. It is necessary to gather up the joint meaning to be found in testimonies of Scripture and Tradition, to interpret them in a new historical situation, and to "translate" their message into the idiom and conceptuality of a new age, so that its content, relevance, and credibility shine forth. Pope John

---

[1] The non-existence of any post-apostolic public revelation, already taught at Vatican I (*DS* 3020, 3070), was reiterated in the anti-Modernist decree *Lamentabili* (1907, *DS* 3421).

XXIII, in his opening allocution at Vatican II, stressed the pastoral importance of presenting the faith in a way demanded by our own times.[2] Paul VI likewise asserted: "Nowadays a serious effort is required of us to ensure that the teaching of the faith should keep the fullness of its meaning and force, while expressing itself in a form which allows it to reach the spirit and heart of the people to whom it is addressed."[3]

These exhortations, however, do not mean that the terminology of councils should be casually abandoned. Pius XII in *Humani generis* (1950) taught that although the Church had not always used the same terms in the same way, the language of the Church's dogma and the common terminology of the schools, hammered out over the course of centuries, was grounded in the reality itself (*DS* 3883). Paul VI, in his encyclical *Mysterium Fidei* (1965), made a similar statement:

> Who indeed would ever tolerate that the dogmatic formulas used by the ecumenical councils for the mysteries of the Most Blessed Trinity and the Incarnation be judged as no longer appropriate for men of our times and therefore permit others to be rashly substituted for them? Likewise, it cannot be tolerated that any individual should on his own authority modify the formulas used by the Council of Trent to express belief in eucharistic mystery. These formulas, like the others which the Church uses to propose the

---

[2] The Abbott edition of *The Documents of Vatican II*, following the Latin text released by the Vatican Press Office, quotes John XXIII as saying on October 11, 1962: "The substance of the doctrine of the deposit of faith is one thing, and the way in which it is presented is another" (New York: America Press, 1966), 715. The official version subsequently published adds to the sentence: "keeping the same sense and the same meaning" *(eodem tamen sensu eademque sententia)*. See Sacrosanctum Oecumenicum Concilium Vaticanum II, *Constitutiones, Decreta, Declarationes* (Vatican City: Typis Polyglottis Vaticanis, 1966), 854–72, at 865; also *AAS* (1962): 786–96, at 792.

[3] Paul VI, Apostolic Exhortation, "Quinque iam anni," *AAS* 63 (1971): 100–1.

dogmas of faith, express concepts that are not tied to a certain form of human culture, or to a specific phase of scientific progress, or one or other theological school. No, these formulas present that part of reality which necessary and universal experience permits the human mind to grasp and to manifest with exact terms taken from either common or polished language. For this reason, these formulas are adapted to men of all times and all places. (§24)

There is no need to deny that the Magisterium sometimes uses mutable human concepts to convey transcendent truth. The Congregation for the Doctrine of the Faith stated in 1973: "Even though the truths which the Church intends to teach through her dogmatic formulas are distinct from the changeable conceptions of a given epoch and can be expressed without them, nevertheless it can sometimes happen that these truths may be enunciated by the sacred Magisterium in terms that bear traces of such conceptions."[4] With the passage of years and the shifts in human culture, it may become necessary to explain the terms or even, in some cases, to replace them. But efforts should be made to retain continuity so that the ancient documents may still be intelligible.

The second function of the Magisterium is the negative one whereby the hierarchical authorities, as judges, defend the faith against opposed errors. Until relatively recent times, the doctrinal decrees of the Magisterium were predominantly concerned with warding off heresy, sometimes under pain of a solemn excommunication, called an "anathema."[5] In condemning misinterpretations of the faith, the Magisterium inevitably gives a more precise

---

[4] Congregation for the Doctrine of the Faith, *Mysterium Ecclesiae, AAS* 65 (1973): 396–408, at 403. English translation, "Declaration in Defense of the Catholic Doctrine of the Church Against Certain Errors of the Present Day," *Origins* 3 (1973): 97, 99–100, 110–12, at 110–11.

[5] The term "anathema" in the Hebrew Scriptures often refers to a curse, setting a person or thing apart for destruction. In 1 Corinthians 16:22 and Galatians 1:8–9, St. Paul used the word to denote separation from the Christian community or excommunication. In the early councils the term was regularly used in condemnations of heresy, a practice that still

interpretation to what has been handed down in the doctrinal tradition, and thus "develops" the doctrine.

The Magisterium consequently has a third function: to clarify the faith by bringing forth from the treasury "things new and old." In answering new questions, as in refuting new errors, the Magisterium sometimes brings out hitherto unnoticed implications of the faith. The idea of dogmatic development will be considered later in this chapter.

APPLYING THE FAITH TO LIFE

Vatican II, as we have seen, teaches that the Magisterium must proclaim what is to be believed in faith and applied in practice (*fidem credendam et moribus applicandam*). This language echoes the coupling of faith and morals in many magisterial documents (*res fidei et morum*). The term *mores*—here translated "morals"—takes on different nuances in different documents. It often means something like "patterns of behavior commended by the gospel."[6]

Since ancient times the Magisterium has been accustomed to lay down rules of conduct for individuals seeking to be faithful to the law of God and to the gospel of Christ. These rules are not arbitrary decisions of the Church but applications of what Paul would call "the law of Christ" (1 Cor 9:21; Gal 6:2).

In her social teaching the Church goes beyond individual morality and speaks out on public affairs, seeking to promote the dignity of the human person and the common good. Since Pope Leo XIII published his encyclical *Rerum novarum* in 1891, a series

---

continued as late as Vatican I. The 1917 Code of Canon Law treats anathematization as a solemn excommunication (c. 2257 §2). The Code of 1983, however, makes no reference to anathemas.

6 Sullivan, profiting from the research of Maurice Bévenot, points out that the term *mores*, particularly in the decrees of Trent, includes more than what we mean by morality. He would prefer to translate it by "matters of Christian practice" based on the gospel. See Sullivan, *Magisterium,* 128–29.

of popes and the Second Vatican Council have built up a coherent body of Christian social teaching and have occasionally made specific applications to current affairs. The *Compendium of the Social Doctrine of the Church* (2005) indicates that such social teaching has true authority:

> Insofar as it is part of the Church's moral teaching, the Church's social doctrine has the same dignity and authority as her moral teaching. It is authentic Magisterium, which obligates the faithful to adhere to it. The doctrinal weight of the different teachings and the assent required are determined by the nature of the particular teachings, by their level of independence from contingent and variable elements, and by the frequency with which they are invoked. (§80)

In the sociopolitical area the Church's mission is not to make pronouncements on the technical aspects of politics, economics, and the social sciences, but to illuminate the moral and religious dimensions of social questions so that the faithful may better form their consciences.[7] The value of applications to concrete situations depends in part on the availability of sufficient factual information, on technically correct analysis, and on the human prudence of those making the applications. The applications, therefore, may be less certain than the principles.

INFALLIBILITY OF THE CHURCH AS A WHOLE

The Church, according to Christian belief, is divinely assisted by the Lord, who preserves her in the truth by his Spirit (Jn 14:26, 16:13) and promises to remain with her apostolic leaders until "the close of the age" (Mt 28:20), preventing the powers of death from prevailing against her (Mt 16:18). Convinced that she stands

---

7 See the essays of Johannes Baptist Metz, Edward Schillebeeckx, and others in *Concilium*, vol. 36, *Faith and the World of Politics* (New York: Paulist, 1968); also Francis S. Fiorenza, "The Church's Religious Identity and Its Social and Political Mission," *Theological Studies* 43 (1982): 197–225.

in full institutional continuity with the apostolic Church, the Catholic Church is confident that she will never cease to bear authentic witness to Christ. If the Church as a body were to fall away from the gospel, Christ's promises would be made void, and God would be proved unfaithful.

Together with the promise of perpetuity, Christ has given to the Church means whereby she can assuredly remain "the pillar and the bulwark of the truth" (1 Tim 3:15; cf. 2 Tim 2:19). These means include the canonical Scriptures, as an inspired record of the developing faith of the People of God in its constitutive phase; sacred Tradition, whereby the Church preserves her deposit of faith as a living memory; the sacraments, whereby she encounters the living Lord in faith; prayer, whereby she invokes the Spirit of Truth; and the ecclesiastical office, which continues to shepherd God's People as the needs of the time require.

The perpetuity or indefectibility of the Church as a community of faith involves her preservation from errors that would contradict the gospel. Thanks to the promised assistance of the Holy Spirit and the created means of grace, the Church as a whole has what Vatican II speaks of as a "charism of infallibility" (*LG* 25). Putting this idea in a positive form, one may say that the Church is gifted with what Vatican I calls a "charism of unfailing truth and faith" (*DS* 3071). This does not mean that the faithful or their pastors cannot be mistaken in some of their opinions, but that, to the extent that they are in full communion in the Church, their faith will be unsullied. Thanks especially to the indwelling of the Holy Spirit, the firm and universal agreement of the pastors and the whole body of the faithful about matters of faith and morals cannot be in error (*LG* 12).

INFALLIBILITY OF THE MAGISTERIUM: SUBJECT AND EXERCISE

The Magisterium is one of the means whereby God preserves the Church in the truth of the gospel. In order for the Church to be indefectible it is necessary that those preaching and teaching the faith on the highest authoritative level be not mistaken about what pertains essentially to revelation. According to Catholic belief, as defined at Vatican I and reaffirmed at Vatican II, the supreme Magisterium, in its definitive teaching about matters of faith and morals, is divinely protected against error.

Strictly speaking, infallibility is a property of the Magisterium in its activity of teaching, not a property of magisterial statements. The statements protected by infallibility are said to be "irreformable" (*DS* 3074). In the documents of Vatican I, "irreformable" meant that the statements are not subject to rejection or correction by any other authorities in the Church, as had been held by the Gallicans, who contended that papal definitions were always subject to the judgment of the Church (*DS* 2284). Irreformable statements may, however, require completion, refinement, reinterpretation, and restatement in accordance with new conditions, which raise new questions and provide new information, new conceptual categories, new methods, and new vocabulary. The "irreformability" of a definition, though it rules out subsequent reversals, leaves room for considerable "reformulation."[8] Since Vatican Council II, papal documents often use the term "definitive" in the places where, earlier, one would have expected the term "irreformable." This is notably the case in the Profession of Faith of 1989, in the Code of Canon Law (c. 249), and in the supplement to canon 750 inserted by the Apostolic Letter *Ad tuendam fidem* of May 18, 1998, texts that we shall examine in the next chapter. This change of terminology is attributable to Vatican II, which speaks of "definitive" acts of teaching and of doctrine to which "definitive" assent is to be given (*LG* 25).

The episcopal and papal forms of magisterial infallibility may be separately considered.

---

[8] The problem of the permanence of dogma and the historical relativity of the concepts and language is briefly but carefully treated in *Mysterium Ecclesiae*, sec. 5, *AAS* 65: 402–4; English translation, 110–11.

THE UNIVERSAL MAGISTERIUM
OF THE BISHOPS

The universal Magisterium of the bishops can be exercised in either of two forms, called ordinary and extraordinary (*DS* 3011; *LG* 25). The *ordinary* universal Magisterium is engaged when the whole body of bishops, in hierarchical communion with the successor of Peter, is morally unanimous in teaching a certain doctrine as a matter of divine and Catholic faith, to be accepted by all as pertaining to the faith of the Church. The unanimity of the episcopal body is sometimes difficult to verify, but in many cases it is apparent from what the bishops regularly do or knowingly permit in preaching, liturgical prayer, catechesis, confessional practice, and the like.

Several examples may be instanced. The communion of saints is confessed as a matter of faith in the Apostles' Creed but has never been defined as a dogma. But all bishops, at least in the West, recite and encourage others to recite the Apostles' Creed. In the *Confiteor* of the Roman Mass the faithful invoke "Blessed Mary ever virgin," though the perpetual virginity of Mary has not yet been solemnly defined. Some doctrines were in peaceful possession for a long time and were later solemnly defined by popes or councils. The Immaculate Conception and Assumption of the Blessed Virgin were affirmed in approved prayers and liturgical feasts for many centuries before being defined as papal dogmas in 1854 and 1950, respectively. In a number of cases the pope or the Congregation for the Doctrine of the Faith has authoritatively declared that a given doctrine is contained in the word of God and has been constantly taught by the ordinary universal Magisterium. The ordinary and universal Magisterium, therefore, is by no means an empty category.

The *extraordinary* Magisterium of the bishops comes into play when bishops representing the universal Church, by a united act, solemnly define a matter of faith or morals, with the approval of the pope. The dogmatic definitions of the early councils regarding the Trinity and Christology, and the decrees of Vatican I regarding papal primacy and infallibility, may serve as examples. The ecumenicity of certain early councils (notably the four from Nicaea to Chalcedon, but also the next three, ending with Nicaea II, 787) is generally admitted by Catholics, Orthodox, and Protestants. There is, however, no canonical list of all the ecumenical councils. Following a list that was drawn up by Robert Bellarmine in the seventeenth century, Catholics commonly include the general councils convened by popes in the Middle Ages and accordingly reckon Vatican II as the twenty-first ecumenical council. Western councils such as Trent, Vatican I, and Vatican II clearly claimed to be ecumenical and are accepted as such by the popes. Their solemn teachings, therefore, are for Catholics beyond challenge.

Statements emanating from ecumenical councils are definitive only when the council so indicates. Often the council will indicate its intention to define by using solemn language such as: "This Holy Council believes and confesses . . . ," or by pronouncing an anathema: "If anyone does not confess . . . , let him be anathema." Councils such as Trent and Vatican I often divided their decrees into chapters and canons in such as way that the chapters stated positively the contradictory of what the anathema denied. The teaching of the chapter is definitive at least to the extent that it contradicts the anathema in the canon. But, besides containing defined doctrine, the chapters often contain additional explanatory matter that is not infallibly taught.[9]

Regarding the teachings of Vatican II, the Doctrinal Commission declared:

In view of conciliar practice and the pastoral purposes of the present Council, this sacred Synod defines matters of faith or morals

---

[9] On the authority of the chapters and canons at the Councils of Trent and Vatican I, see Ioachim Salaverri, *De Ecclesia Christi in Sacrae Theologiae Summa,* vol. 1: *Theologiae Fundamentalis,* Part III, nos. 906–13, 811–16.

as binding on the Church only when the Synod itself openly declares so.

Other matters which the sacred Synod proposes as the doctrine of the supreme teaching authority of the Church, each and every member of the faithful is obliged to accept and embrace according to the mind of the sacred Synod itself, which becomes known either from the subject matter or from the language employed, according to the norms of theological interpretation.[10]

Vatican II, as instructed by Pope John XXIII, refrained from defining any new doctrines to be held under pain of heresy. But it did deliberately go beyond previous magisterial statements in affirming that ordination to the episcopate is a sacrament and that the bishops in communion with the successor of Peter constitute a college. The sacramentality of episcopal ordination is, moreover, stated with great emphasis:

This sacred Synod teaches that by episcopal consecration is conferred the fullness of the sacrament of orders, that fullness which in the Church's liturgical practice and in the language of the holy Fathers of the Church is undoubtedly called the high priesthood, the apex of the sacred ministry. (*LG* 21)

Commentators generally agree that while this is not a dogmatic definition in the strict sense, it ranks as a "definitive judgment"[11] and calls for "obligatory adherence."[12] The unanimity of the Fathers

---

10 Declaration of the Theological Commission of March 6, 1964, quoted with approval by the Secretary General of the Council, November 16, 1964; text in *Documents of Vatican II*, ed. Walter M. Abbott (New York: America Press, 1966), 98. The Theological Commission is called in other translations "Doctrinal Commission," a term more closely corresponding to the Latin, *Commissio de Doctrina Fidei et Morum*.

11 Yves Congar, "En guise de conclusion," in Baraúna, *L'Église de Vatican II*, 1365–73, at 1367.

12 Joseph Ratzinger, "La collégialité épiscopale, développement théologique," in Baraúna, *L'Église de Vatican II*, 763–90, at 789.

voting for chapter III of *Lumen gentium* would seem sufficient for the affirmation here quoted to be considered at least as an utterance of the ordinary universal Magisterium, confirmed by the pope.

PAPAL MAGISTERIUM: ORDINARY AND EXTRAORDINARY

Like the bishops, the pope has an ordinary and an extraordinary Magisterium.[13] He exercises his *ordinary* Magisterium in his day-to-day preaching and in written statements that do not claim to enjoy the guarantee of infallibility. Encyclical letters are normally addressed by the pope to the entire episcopate or the entire world. Encyclicals have rarely if ever been used to define new dogmas, though they frequently reaffirm doctrines that are already matters of faith. An encyclical, therefore, is an expression of the pope's ordinary teaching authority, which, according to the common teaching, is not infallible. The same may be said of apostolic exhortations, letters to priests, allocutions, messages, homilies, and the like.

The pope makes use of his *extraordinary* Magisterium when he issues an ex cathedra pronouncement, as occurred when Pius IX defined the Immaculate Conception of the Blessed Virgin Mary in 1854 (*DS* 2803) and when Pius XII defined the Assumption of the Blessed Virgin in 1950 (*DS* 3903). In explaining the infallibility of such definitions, Vatican I laid down several conditions or limitations. The pope's teaching is infallible only when he speaks (a) "in the chair of Peter," using his full apostolic authority, (b) concerning a doctrine of faith or morals *(doctrina de fide vel moribus)*, and (c) defining what must be held as a matter of faith by all members of the Church. The infallibility of such definitions is attributed to the divine assistance promised to the pope in the

---

[13] For an overview of various types of papal pronouncement, see Francis G. Morrisey, *Papal and Curial Pronouncements: Their Canonical Significance in Light of the Code of Canon Law,* 2d ed. (Ottawa: St. Paul University, Faculty of Canon Law, 2001), 9–20.

person of Peter (*DS* 3074). When the pope defines a dogma or performs a particularly solemn act he normally uses an Apostolic Constitution, in the form of a bull.

Except for the definition of the Immaculate Conception, there is little clarity about which papal statements prior to Vatican I are irreformable. Most authors would agree on about half a dozen statements. Among the clearest examples are the statement of Pope Benedict XII on the nature of the beatific vision (1336; *DS* 1000–2) and the condemnation of five Jansenist propositions by Innocent X (1653; *DS* 2001–7).[14]

The bare text of the Vatican I definition, taken without regard to the Council's accompanying explanation, could be misunderstood as giving absolute powers to the pope to define whatever he chooses. But when the definition is read in continuity with the preceding paragraphs, and especially in the light of the *relatio* given to the council fathers by Bishop Gasser on behalf of the Deputation on Faith,[15] it is apparent that the pope cannot define except under certain specified conditions. He must be expressing, defending, or explaining the word of God as contained in Scripture or apostolic Tradition and held by the Church throughout the centuries. In their reply to Bismarck, already mentioned in chapter 3, the German bishops pointed out that papal infallibility is limited insofar as he cannot contradict the teaching of Scripture and Tradition and the previous definitions of the Magisterium.[16]

---

14 For discussion of doctrinal definitions in papal documents, see Francis A. Sullivan, *Creative Fidelity: Weighing and Interpreting Documents of the Magisterium* (New York: Paulist, 1996), 80–92.

15 As mentioned in chapter 5, Gasser's *Relatio* is printed in Mansi 52:1204–32; translation and commentary in James T. O'Connor, *The Gift of Infallibility* (Boston: St. Paul Editions, 1986). For further discussion, see Küng, *Structures of the Church*, 366–77; Gustave Thils, *L'Infaillibilité pontificale* (Gembloux: Duculot, 1969), 186–221; Avery Dulles, "Moderate Infallibilism: An Ecumenical Approach," in *A Church to Believe In* (New York: Crossroad, 1982), 133–48.

16 Collective Declaration of the German Bishops, 1875 (*DS* 3116). Similar statements were made at Vatican II, notably by the Doctrinal Commission;

Picking up on these themes, Vatican II declared that the Magisterium is not above the word of God but serves that word (*DV* 10). The pope in defining doctrine is manifestly bound to the faith of the whole Church, both as taught by his fellow bishops and as lived by the faithful as a body (*LG* 12, 25). Although not juridically dependent on any other agency in the Church, the pope is obliged in the nature of the case to take the necessary means to ascertain the faith of the Church. If the pope did not fulfill these necessary conditions, or if he were heretical, schismatic, demented, or coerced, he could not exercise his teaching authority.[17] Catholics may rest assured that the pope does not issue dogmatic definitions without taking the necessary means to inform himself.

Without appealing to his personal infallibility, the pope can by his ordinary teaching authority "confirm" or "declare" doctrines that were already taught by the ordinary and universal Magisterium on the basis of Scripture and the constant Tradition of the Church. Pope John Paul II did this on several occasions. In his encyclical *Evangelium vitae* (1995) he emphatically taught the grave sinfulness of taking innocent human life (*EV* 57), committing or procuring abortion (*EV* 62), and engaging in euthanasia (*EV* 65). In the same encyclical he explained that he was speaking with the unanimous support of the cardinals and bishops (*EV* 5).

Similarly, in his Apostolic Letter *Ordinatio sacerdotalis* (1994), Pope John Paul II taught that the Church has no authority whatsoever to confer priestly ordination on women, and that this judgment is to be held definitively by all the faithful. The Congregation for the Doctrine of the Faith declared, in a "response" of October 28, 1995, that Pope John Paul II's determination on this point confirmed a teaching that pertained to the deposit of faith and one that had already been taught infallibly by the ordinary and universal

---

see Karl Rahner in Herbert Vorgrimler, ed., *Commentary on the Documents of Vatican II,* vol. 1: Constitution on the Church, chap. 3, 202–3.

[17] See Sullivan, *Magisterium,* 101–2.

Magisterium.[18] Although the response of the CDF is not itself protected by the charism of infallibility, it embodies the considered judgment of the highest doctrinal organ of the Church, confirmed by the pope. In view of the strong evidence from Scripture and Tradition for the reservation of ordination to men, the papal decision is solidly grounded in the deposit of faith.[19]

PRIMARY AND SECONDARY OBJECTS OF INFALLIBILITY

There has been much discussion regarding the object of the infallible Magisterium. Vatican I stated that the purpose of papal infallibility was to enable the popes "religiously to guard and faithfully to expound the revelation or deposit of faith that was handed down through the Apostles" (*DS* 3070). It also stated that papal definitions were infallible only when they dealt with "doctrine of faith and morals" (*doctrina fidei et morum, DS* 3074).

Vatican II likewise stated that the infallibility of the Church in defining doctrine "extends as far as does the deposit of divine revelation, which must be religiously guarded and faithfully expounded" (*LG* 25). To clarify this concise statement the Doctrinal Commission at Vatican II provided an explanation: "The object of infallibility extends to all those things, and only to those, which either directly pertain to the deposit itself or are required in order that the same deposit may be religiously safeguarded and faithfully expounded."[20] The Congregation for the

---

[18] Congregation for the Doctrine of the Faith, "Response to *Dubium*," *Origins* 25 (November 30, 1995): 401–5; *AAS* 87 (1995): 1114.

[19] The arguments from Scripture and Tradition, as well as from theological reasoning, are spelled out in the Declaration of the Congregation for the Faith, *"Inter insigniores"* of October 15, 1976; *Origins* 6 (February 3, 1977): 517, 519–24.

[20] "Objectum infallibilitatis . . . extenditur at ea omnia, et ad ea tantum, quae vel directe ad ipsum depositum revelatum spectant, vel quae ad idem depositum sancte custodiendum et fideliter exponendum requiruntur, ut

Doctrine of the Faith, in its 1973 Declaration, *Mysterium Ecclesiae,* used similar terms:

> According to Catholic doctrine the infallibility of the magisterium of the Church extends not only to the deposit of faith but also to those things without which this deposit cannot be properly safeguarded and explained. However, the extension of this infallibility to the deposit of faith itself is a truth that the Church has from the beginning held as being certainly revealed in the promises of Christ. (§3)

Theologians accordingly distinguish between the primary object of infallibility, the deposit of revelation itself, and the secondary object, whatever is required to defend and expound the deposit. The extension of infallibility to the primary object is a matter of faith; its extension to the secondary object is theologically certain Catholic teaching.

The line of demarcation between the primary and secondary objects is not always easy to draw, because the primary object has a capacity for expansion as new implications come to be recognized in the original deposit. When the Magisterium, in calling for definitive assent to a certain doctrine, does not clearly indicate whether it is teaching a revealed truth, theologians may have different views about whether the teaching was always contained in the deposit of faith or whether it is being taught as an additional truth inseparably connected with revelation.

DEVELOPMENT OF DOCTRINE

As stated above, the faith contained in the deposit must sometimes be proclaimed in new formulations in order to obviate misunderstandings or make the message intelligible and credible in

---

habetur in Conc. Vat I: *DS* 3070 (1836), ubi de infallibilitate Romani Pontificis," *Acta Synodalia* III/8 (Vatican City: Libreria Editrice Vaticana, 1970), 89.

new cultures. New dogmas, if they state no more than was formally implied in the original revelation, fall within the primary object of magisterial infallibility. The Council of Nicaea, for example, used the term *homoousion* ("consubstantial") to express a revealed truth that some theologians had overlooked: the full divinity of the Son and his unity with the Father in the same identical divine nature. This process of reformulation results in the development of dogma.

In the early twentieth century there was an inconclusive debate about whether the Church can dogmatically define what is only "virtually" rather than "formally" revealed. By the "virtually revealed" was meant something that can indeed be deduced from revelation, but only with the help of truths naturally known. An example of such a deduction is given by Matthias J. Scheeben: "God the Father and the Son have the same nature in common [revealed]; but nature is the proximate principle of activity [naturally known]; hence they have a common activity *ad extra*."[21] Can such a conclusion be proclaimed as a revealed truth?

If revelation is understood propositionally, as it was by most parties to the dispute, it would seem that the conclusion could not be imposed in the name of revelation, for, according to an established axiom of logic, the conclusion can have no greater certainty than the weaker premise. But if revelation is understood in terms of a broader theory of communication, which admits that a speaker may in the act of speaking communicate more than is propositionally contained in the meaning of the words used, a conclusion achieved with the help of premises not themselves revealed may say no more than was really (though non-propositionally) communicated in the original event of revelation. As Karl Rahner points out, statements of revelation, as salvific events, communicate *(mitteilen)* more than they formally state. Hence the Magisterium,

---

[21] Matthias J. Scheeben, *Handbuch der katholische Dogmatik,* vol. 1 (Freiburg: Herder, 1873), 30.

when it explicates revelation, may infallibly teach doctrines that, in terms of formal logic, were only virtually implicit in the deposit.[22] This does not mean, however, that all theological conclusions are definable.

In ancient times, the Magisterium did not seek to define the implications of revelation except to the degree that was considered necessary to defend the faith against heretical distortions. Only with great reluctance did the Fathers at Nicaea, for example, insert the non-biblical term *homoousion* ("consubstantial") into the creed. But in recent times, especially in the period between 1850 and 1950, the Roman Magisterium deliberately engaged in the process of dogmatic development. Dogmas such as the Immaculate Conception and the Assumption of the Blessed Virgin (defined respectively Pius IX and Pius XII) were intended to enrich the faith and piety of Catholics in a positive way, and to redound to the honor and glory of God, rather than to avert specific threats to the faith. This period of the "extensive" development of dogma seems to have peaked and subsided, at least for the time being, though some Catholics are still asking for dogmatic definitions of new Marian titles and privileges. Vatican II, following the instructions of Pope John XXIII, abstained from invoking its own infallibility. It neither defined new dogmas nor anathematized new errors. No pope since Vatican II has as yet made an ex cathedra definition, but Pope John Paul II affirmed that the pope has the power to do so under the conditions laid down by Vatican I (*UUS* 94).

Secondary Objects of Infallibility

The extent of the secondary object of magisterial infallibility is thoroughly discussed in the standard theological manuals.[23]

---

[22] Karl Rahner, "The Development of Dogma," *Theological Investigations,* vol. 1 (Baltimore: Helicon, 1961), 39–78, esp. 68–75.

[23] Salaverri, *De Ecclesia Christi* §§698–737, 729–47; Sullivan, *Magisterium,* 131–52.

Where competent authorities disagree about whether a given doctrine is infallibly taught, the burden of proof rests juridically on those who contend for infallibility. For, according to the principles of canon law, a doubtfully infallible definition is in practice to be treated as though it were non-infallible (CIC, c. 749, #3).

All agree that the secondary object includes whatever must be believed as a necessary condition or necessary consequence of the assent to revelation itself. Very often the crucial question is whether the doctrine in question is not merely useful but truly indispensable for the exposition and defense of the apostolic revelation, as Vatican II and the CDF Declaration *Mysterium Ecclesiae* seem to require.

It is generally agreed that the Magisterium can infallibly declare the "preambles of faith," that is, naturally knowable truths implied in the credibility of the Christian message, such as the capacity of the human mind to grasp truth about invisible realities, to know the existence of God by reasoning from the created world (*DS* 3004, 3026, 3538), and to grasp the possibility of revelation (*DS* 3027) and miracles (*DS* 3033–34).

A strong case for infallibility can be made in the case of certain facts closely connected with the truth of revelation (called "dogmatic facts") such as the ecumenical authority of a given council or the validity of the election of a given pope, since this information might be essential to establish the validity of a dogmatic definition. Unless the Church could identify her popes and ecumenical councils with full authority, her dogmatic teaching would be clouded by doubt.

About other secondary objects there are differences of opinion. The extension of infallibility to "dogmatic facts" became a burning issue when Cornelius Jansen was condemned for having taught five propositions that according to his followers were incorrectly ascribed to him (*DS* 2001–7). The Holy See insisted that Jansen himself taught the propositions in the sense that it had rejected (*DS* 2010–12; 2020). But even if Jansen understood his propositions in an orthodox sense, it cannot be denied that the Magisterium had the competence to condemn the propositions according to the normal meaning of the words. What Jansen had in mind is a more complicated question.

Among other non-revealed matters that have frequently been seen as falling within the secondary object of infallibility is the solemn canonization of saints.[24] Some authors defend, in addition, a kind of "practical infallibility" in papal actions such as the approval of religious institutes. Although the common teaching of theologians gives some support for holding infallibility in these cases, it is difficult to see how they fit under the object of infallibility as defined by the two Vatican Councils.

Moral theologians debate about the competence of the Magisterium to speak definitively in its teaching concerning the natural law. They generally agree that, as Francis Sullivan puts it, "some of the basic principles of the natural law are also formally revealed, and as such, belong to the primary object of infallible magisterium."[25] The Ten Commandments, for example, are little more

---

[24] The Catholic participants to the United States Lutheran-Catholic Dialogue, in their reflections on infallible teaching, wrote: "The theological manuals of recent generations rather commonly hold that solemn canonizations of saints, as contained in papal decretal letters, are infallible. The tradition in favor of infallibility in the matter has been traced back at least to the time of Thomas Aquinas, but there are genuine difficulties in seeing how canonizations fall within the object of papal infallibility as taught by Vatican I or Vatican II. Certainly, the virtues of particular persons of post-biblical times, and their present situation before God, can scarcely be reckoned as part of the apostolic deposit of faith. . . . The Church has the power to recognize authentic Christian holiness, yet canonization would not seem of its nature to convey infallible certitude that the holiness in question was actually present in the life of this or that historical person" (§32). References to literature on canonizations are given in the footnotes, which I have not reproduced here. See "Roman Catholic Reflections," in *Teaching Authority and Infallibility in the Church*, ed. Empie et al., 49–50.

[25] Sullivan, *Magisterium,* 149.

than a restatement for Israelites of the requirements of the natural law. In *Evangelium vitae* Pope John Paul II bases his teaching on the inviolability of innocent human life on natural law "reaffirmed by Sacred Scripture," as well as by Tradition and the Magisterium (*EV* 57).

At a conference with Cardinal Ratzinger and other representatives of the CDF and several Committees on Doctrine, Archbishop Daniel Pilarczyk, as chairman of the Committee on Doctrine of the United States Conference of Catholic bishops, remarked:

> Further clarification about the Church's ability to teach matters of natural law infallibly would be desirable. According to one opinion, the capacity to teach the natural law with full authority falls within the Church's mission, since the observance of the natural law is required for salvation. According to another opinion, the magisterium can speak with pastoral authority on all issues of the moral law. It can also speak infallibly on basic principles of the natural law that are also formally revealed; but the Church, it is said, has no power to speak infallibly about particular applications of the natural moral law unless these can be shown to be intimately or necessarily connected with revelation.[26]

---

26 Daniel E. Pilarczyk, "The Role of the Theologian in a Catholic College or University in the Light of *Ad tuendam fidem* and the *Professio fidei*," in *Proclaiming the Truth of Jesus Christ: Papers from the Vallombrosa Meeting* (Washington, DC: United States Catholic Conference, 2000), 69–82, at 80. As holding the first opinion (that all matters of natural law fall within the object of irreformable definitions), Pilarczyk quoted from Umberto Betti, commenting on the 1989 Profession of Faith in *L'Osservatore Romano* (English-language edition), 13 March 1989, 4. As a representative of the second opinion, requiring intimate connection with revelation, he cited an article by Francis A. Sullivan, "Some Observations on the New Formula for the Profession of Faith," in *Gregorianum* 70 (1989): 552–54. In his *Magisterium*, 136–52, Sullivan takes the same position. In footnote 46, 227, Sullivan lists a considerable number of prominent moral theologians who hold that particular norms of the natural law "are not proper matter of irreformable teaching."

The response of the CDF was carefully worded. It distinguished between negative and positive norms. "Given that the observance of all negative moral norms that concern intrinsically evil acts *(intrinsece mala)* is necessary for salvation, it follows that the Magisterium has the competence to teach infallibly and make obligatory the definitive assent of the members of the faithful with regard to the knowledge and application in life of these norms. This judgment belongs to the Catholic doctrine on the infallibility of the Magisterium."

Turning then to positive norms, the CDF stated: "With regard to the particular applications of the norms of the natural moral law that do not have a necessary connection with Revelation—for example, numerous positive moral norms that are valid *ut in pluribus*—it has not been defined nor is it binding that the Magisterium can teach infallibly in such specific matters."[27]

Francis Sullivan interprets John Paul II's position as opposed to his own. The encyclical *Veritatis splendor* (1993), as he understands it, implies that all moral truths, including those of the natural order, are knowable from revelation. If so, says Sullivan, the entire moral law could be seen as falling within the primary object of infallibility.[28]

The pope, we may agree, teaches in *Veritatis splendor* that the entire moral law is better understood in the light of revelation, as contained in Holy Scripture and Tradition (*VS* 5, 28, and so on). In *Evangelium vitae* he condemned murder, abortion, and euthanasia on the basis of the teaching of the ordinary and universal Magisterium. He stated that the teaching of the Magisterium was supported by Scripture as well as by the natural law.

---

27 CDF Representatives, "Some Brief Responses to Questions Regarding the *Professio fidei*," *Proclaiming the Truth of Jesus Christ: Papers from the Vallombrosa Meeting*, 61–66, at 66.

28 Francis A. Sullivan, "Infallible Teaching on Moral Issues? Reflections on *Veritatis splendor* and *Evangelium vitae*," in *Choosing Life: A Dialogue on Evangelium vitae*, ed. Kevin W. Wildes and Alan Mitchell (Washington, DC: Georgetown University Press, 1997), 77–89.

But it is not evident that he meant to say that all precepts of the natural moral law are revealed truths, falling within the primary object of infallibility. As we shall see in our next chapter, the CDF classifies some teachings of the moral law as belonging to the secondary object of infallibility.

CHAPTER SEVEN

■ ■ ■

The Response Due
to the Magisterium

THEOLOGICAL NOTES

IN THE MANUALS published before and during Vatican II, it was customary to attach theological notes or qualifications to every proposition being taught.[1] Was it a matter of faith, to be believed by all under pain of heresy, or did it have some lesser degree of obligatory force? These theological notes depended primarily on the degree to which the Magisterium had engaged its authority. A very simplified list would include the following:

1. Doctrine of faith
    a. defined (by pope or council)
    b. taught by the ordinary and universal Magisterium
2. Doctrine infallibly taught as inseparably connected with revelation
3. Doctrine authoritatively but non-infallibly taught by Magisterium

---

[1] Ioachim Salaverri, in the treatise *De Ecclesia* of the multivolume *Sacrae Theologiae Summa*, lists fourteen theological "notes" used in the series, with the "censures" of errors opposed to each; vol. 1, §§884–905; 800–10. For a full discussion of theological notes, see Sisto Cartechini, *Dall'Opinione al Domma: Valore delle Note teologiche* (Rome: Civiltà Cattolica, 1953).

4. Theological conclusion logically deduced from a proposition of faith

5. Probable opinion

In the decade following the council these theological notes disappeared from textbooks. There was a period of confusion as to what doctrines were binding, on what grounds, and in what measure. Some theologians acted as though it were acceptable for Catholics to contest every doctrine of the Church that had not been solemnly defined. A few authors contended that since revelation was not originally given as a set of propositions, no Christian should be required to subscribe to any propositions as matters of faith. Or alternatively, the doctrines of the Church were regarded as being so historically and culturally conditioned that none of them could be classified as revealed or irreversibly true. Individuals were at times encouraged to construct creeds and confessions of their own, thus blurring the contours of the Church as a visible, universal, and abiding community of faith.

POST-CONCILIAR CLARIFICATIONS

To remedy the growing confusion, the Holy See took a series of steps, several of which may be mentioned here. In 1968 Pope Paul VI, preoccupied by "the disquiet which at the present time agitates certain quarters with regard to the faith," promulgated a profession of faith popularly known as "the Credo of the People of God." While expressly declaring that it was not a dogmatic definition, the pope incorporated in it the substance of the creed of Nicaea, together with some teachings of later councils, notably the teaching of Trent with regard to original sin and the Eucharist, which was being questioned in some circles.[2]

---

[2] Paul VI, "Profession of Faith," in Jacques Dupuis, ed., *The Christian Faith in the Doctrinal Documents of the Catholic Church,* 6th ed. (Staten Island, NY: Alba House, 1996), §39, 24–31.

In 1973 the Congregation for the Doctrine of the Faith published the Declaration *Mysterium Ecclesiae*, dealing primarily with the infallibility of the Magisterium, in response to questions raised by Hans Küng and others. In 1983, the pope promulgated the revised Code of Canon Law, which contained a long section on the Church's Teaching Office *(Munus Docendi)* in canons 747–843.

The Extraordinary Assembly of the Synod of Bishops in 1985 asked Pope John Paul II to draw up a universal catechism. The *Catechism of the Catholic Church* was accordingly composed and published in 1992, with a definitive Latin edition in 1997. Pope John Paul II in the Apostolic Constitution promulgating the *Catechism* declared it to be "a sure norm for teaching the faith and thus a valid and legitimate instrument for ecclesial communion."[3] The various teachings in the *Catechism* have no greater authority than they had in the documents from which they are drawn.[4]

THE PROFESSION OF FAITH OF 1989

In 1989 the Congregation for the Doctrine of the Faith published a new Profession of Faith.[5] It replaced the much briefer Profession of Faith of 1967, which had itself replaced the Tridentine Profession of Faith (1564) together with the addition inserted into it in 1877, based on Vatican I, as well as the Oath against Modernism of 1910. The Profession of 1989, currently in force, is designed to reflect the teaching of Vatican II, especially in *Lumen gentium* 25. After the Nicene-Constantinopolitan Creed, which had traditionally stood at

---

3 John Paul II, Apostolic Constitution *Fidei Depositum*, §3, in *Catechism of the Catholic Church*, 2d ed. (Vatican City: Libreria Editrice Vaticana, 2000), 5.

4 "The individual doctrines that the Catechism affirms have no other authority than that which they already possess," wrote Cardinal Joseph Ratzinger in "The *Catechism of the Catholic Church* and the Optimism of the Redeemed," *Communio: International Catholic Review* 20 (1993): 469–84, at 479.

5 Congregation for the Doctrine of the Faith, "Profession of Faith," *Origins* 18 (March 16, 1989): 661, 663.

the head of professions of faith, the Profession of 1989 contains
three added paragraphs, the first dealing with revealed truths, the
second with doctrines definitively taught as inseparably connected
with revelation, and the third with authoritative teachings that are
neither revealed nor inseparably connected with revelation, which
consequently are not definitive.

In May 1998 Pope John Paul II in the motu proprio *Ad tuendam fidem* amended the Code of Canon Law by two small additions to take care of the doctrines treated in the second added
paragraph of the Profession of Faith, which lacked any recognition in the Code of 1983.[6] Using the publication of *Ad tuendam*
as the occasion, Cardinal Joseph Ratzinger, as Prefect of the Congregation for the Doctrine of the Faith, together with Archbishop
Tarcisio Bertone, Secretary of the Congregation, issued a joint
commentary on the three concluding paragraphs of the Profession
of Faith.[7] Relying principally on the new Profession of Faith and
the two documents of 1998, we may at this point consider the
proper responses to doctrinal pronouncements of different types.

The Catholic Church recognizes two creeds as having uncon-
testable authority: the Apostles' Creed and the Nicene-Constantinopolitan Creed.[8] The Apostles' Creed, which differs hardly at all

---

[6] John Paul II, Apostolic Letter motu proprio, *"Ad tuendam fidem,"* Origins 28 (July 16, 1998): 113, 115–16. The additions are to canons 750
and 1371 of the CIC and corresponding articles of the Code for Eastern
Churches.

[7] Joseph Ratzinger and Tarcisio Bertone, "Commentary on the Profession
of Faith's Concluding Paragraphs," *Origins* 28 (July 16, 1998): 116–19.
This commentary, since it does not emanate from the Congregation as
such, is not an official document of the Church. Cardinal Ratzinger, however, later explained that the text was composed by the Congregation as a
whole and approved by the cardinals in assembly and also by the pope. It
is not therefore a merely private document. See Joseph Ratzinger, "Stellungnahme," *Stimmen der Zeit* 217 (1999): 168–71, at 171.

[8] The Athanasian Creed (also known as the *Quicumque*) is sometimes
listed as the "third ecumenical creed," but it is not recognized in the East,
and even in the West does not have the same standing as the other two.

from the Roman Creed of the fourth century, remains the creed professed by candidates for baptism in the Roman rite. The Nicene-Constantinopolitan Creed, as its name suggests, is a reworking of the Creed of Nicaea (325) by the Council of Constantinople (381). Popularly known as the Nicene Creed, it has become the baptismal creed of the Eastern churches and is often sung at Mass in churches of the Roman rite. These two creeds are to be accepted by all Catholics as summaries of the key articles of Christian faith.

In its Western or Latin form, the Nicene Creed includes one word that was introduced in the Middle Ages: *Filioque.* This term characterizes the procession of the Holy Spirit as being not only from the Father but also from the Son. Although some theologians question whether the *Filioque* ought to have been introduced into the Creed without prior consultation with the Eastern churches, the teaching expressed by the term has an impressive patristic pedigree and enjoys strong support from the arguments of distinguished theologians. The ecumenical councils of Lyons II (*DS* 850) and Florence (*DS* 1300) solemnly taught the truth of the *Filioque.* Catholics, therefore, should have no hesitation in professing the Creed with the added term, as set forth in the Profession of Faith.

After these preliminary remarks on the Creed we may now turn to the three added paragraphs.

THE FIRST ADDED PARAGRAPH

The first added paragraph concerns doctrines contained in the word of God, handed down in Tradition, and proposed by the

---

It appears in the Lutheran Book of Concord and in the Anglican Book of Common Prayer. Before Vatican II Catholics regularly recited it in the Divine Office for Sundays, but it was eliminated in the revision of the Liturgy of the Hours after the council. Certainly not composed by Athanasius, it is a Western creed probably composed in Southern Gaul about the fifth century. It eloquently and emphatically sets forth the mysteries of the Holy Trinity and the Incarnation in opposition to various ancient heresies.

Church as revealed truths. This category includes both solemn teachings of popes or councils and teachings of the ordinary and universal Magisterium.

According to the Profession of Faith the proper response to such teaching in each and every case is one of "firm faith." Vatican I spoke in this connection of "divine and Catholic faith"—divine because the doctrines are contained in the word of God; Catholic because they are proposed as such by the Catholic Church. The scope of divine and Catholic faith was succinctly stated by Vatican I as including "all those truths which are contained in Scripture and Tradition and which the Church, either by solemn judgment or by her ordinary and universal magisterium, proposes for belief (*credenda*) as having been divinely revealed" (*DS* 3011).

Obstinate denial or obstinate doubt of any doctrine of the Catholic faith is a sin of heresy. It makes one liable to the canonical penalties specified for heresy, including excommunication (CIC, cc. 751, 1364, and so on).

As examples of revealed truths contained in the deposit of faith one could adduce any dogmas defined by ecumenical councils, such as the Real Presence or papal infallibility, or by popes speaking ex cathedra, such as the two Marian dogmas defined in recent centuries. As an example of a revealed truth that has not been solemnly proclaimed, the Ratzinger-Bertone Commentary mentions the doctrine that the voluntary and direct killing of innocent human beings is gravely sinful (*EV* 57).

THE SECOND ADDED PARAGRAPH

The second added paragraph deals with other doctrines pertaining to faith and morals that are proposed by the Church definitively (*definitive*). This category has to do with non-revealed truths that are "required for the sacred presentation and faithful explanation" of the deposit of the faith (canon 750, §2). As we have seen in chapter 6, these doctrines belong to the secondary or indirect object of infallibility. With regard to each and every such teaching, says the Profession of Faith, the proper response is to accept and hold it with a firm and irrevocable assent. In saying "hold" rather than "believe" the Profession of Faith here follows the language of Vatican I, which distinguished between *credenda* (doctrines "to be believed" in the strict sense of the word, *DS* 3011) and *tenenda* (doctrines "to be held," *DS* 3074). Only revealed truths can be in the strict sense believed. The assent to non-revealed truths that are definitively taught must be definitive so as to correspond to the firmness of the teaching.

Many theologians speak in this connection of "ecclesiastical faith"—faith that goes out not directly to God as witness, but to the Church as divinely assisted teacher. This use of the term "ecclesiastical faith" is relatively recent, and is regarded by some as confusing or unsatisfactory.[9] Yet it should be recognized that confidence in the judgment of the Church is involved in the acceptance of the *tenenda*.

The Ratzinger-Bertone Commentary on the new Profession of Faith distinguishes between two types of doctrine in this category: those connected with revelation by logical and by historical necessity. As examples of doctrines connected by logical necessity the Commentary lists several moral doctrines such as the illicitness of euthanasia (*EV* 65), which is infallibly taught though it does not seem to be mentioned in Scripture. The Commentary, therefore, does not treat the entire moral law as falling within the *primary* object of infallibility.

---

[9] The majority of pre–Vatican II theological manuals admitted the concept of "ecclesiastical faith," but some very distinguished authors (including Francisco Marín-Sola, Ambroise Gardeil, and Charles Journet) opposed it. See the discussion in Salaverri, *"De Ecclesia Christi,"* §899, 807–8, and that of Yves Congar in his *Sainte Église* (Paris: Cerf, 1963), 357–73. Since Vatican II Henri de Lubac vigorously criticized the modern use of the term "ecclesiastical faith," holding that the term ought to mean the faith of the Church, pure and simple. See his *The Splendor of the Church* (San Francisco: Ignatius, 1986), 42.

The reservation of priestly orders to men, also mentioned as logically connected with revelation, is a different type of doctrine since, unlike the examples just given, it is not a matter of natural law known by reason. It cannot be known otherwise than by faith in Holy Scripture and Catholic Tradition. In a response of 1995, the CDF officially ruled that this doctrine was infallibly taught by the Magisterium and pertained to the deposit of faith.[10] The 1998 Commentary explains that although the doctrine has been "set forth infallibly by the ordinary and universal Magisterium," it may be understood not as revealed but as logically connected with revelation. But the authors add: "This does not foreclose the possibility that in the future the Church might progress to the point where this teaching could be defined as a doctrine to be believed as divinely revealed" (§11). Such a reclassification, according to the Commentary, would not be unprecedented. The universal jurisdiction and infallibility of the pope, previously understood as logical consequences of revelation, have been regarded as revealed truths since Vatican I.[11]

As examples of truths connected with the deposit of faith by historical necessity the Ratzinger-Bertone Commentary suggests

---

[10] Congregation for the Doctrine of the Faith, "Response to *Dubium*," 401, 403.

[11] At a meeting between the chairmen of several episcopal doctrinal commissions and representatives of the CDF held in Vallombrosa, California, in 1999, Archbishop Daniel Pilarczyk asked whether the teaching of *Ordinatio sacerdotalis* on the ordination of women to the priesthood could be considered a revealed truth, belonging to the first added paragraph of the Profession of Faith. The representatives of the CDF responded that the doctrine could legitimately be regarded as a doctrine of divine and Catholic faith; "for the moment, however, the Magisterium has simply reaffirmed it as a truth of the Church's doctrine (the second paragraph), based on Scripture, attested to and applied in the uninterrupted Tradition, and taught by the ordinary and universal Magisterium, without declaring it to be a dogma that is divinely revealed." See *Proclaiming the Truth of Jesus Christ: Papers from the Vallombrosa Meeting* (Washington, DC: United States Catholic Conference, 2000), 64–65 (CDF) and 79–80 (Pilarczyk).

the validity of papal elections, the ecumenicity of councils, canonizations of saints, and the invalidity of Anglican orders, as declared by Pope Leo XIII in 1896 (*DS* 3315–19). As mentioned in chapter 6, it is not easy to see how the fact that this or that saint possessed heroic virtue is either a necessary condition or a necessary consequence of Christian faith. Since Vatican II, moreover, there have been new debates about the possibility of recognizing Anglican orders. In proposing these two examples, the Commentary presumably intends to recall what is been taught, not to settle current controversies.[12]

In *Ad tuendam fidem* Pope John Paul II states that anyone who rejects propositions falling within the second added paragraph of the Profession of Faith "is opposed to the doctrine of the Catholic Church." If such a person fails to make a retraction after having been admonished by the Apostolic See or by the ordinary, he shall be "punished with a just penalty." The Ratzinger-Bertone Commentary says of such persons that they are "no longer in full communion with the Church."[13]

THE THIRD ADDED PARAGRAPH

The third added paragraph has reference to teachings that are authoritative but are not set forth as definitive. This category is a

---

[12] At the Vallombrosa meeting mentioned in the preceding note, the representatives of the CDF explained that in proposing these dogmatic facts as doctrines to be definitively held, the Magisterium relies "on its faith in the Holy Spirit's assistance to the Church and on the Catholic doctrine of the infallibility of the Magisterium," ibid., 63. Cardinal Ratzinger has written: "The listing of some doctrinal examples as examples does not grant them any other weight than what they had before." See Ratzinger, "Stellungnahme," 17.

[13] Ratzinger-Bertone, "Commentary," §6, 117. In answer to the question whether this lack of full communion with the Church entailed exclusion from the sacraments (Pilarczyk, 81), the representatives of the CDF at the Vallombrosa meeting replied: "Negative," while calling attention to the power of the bishop to impose "just penalties" (*Vallombrosa Papers,* 66).

very broad one, including many types of doctrines that can lead to a better understanding of faith and morality. Pius XII in *Humani generis* discussed the kind of response that is due to non-infallible authoritative teaching of the papal Magisterium (*DS* 3885). He declared:

> 20. Nor must it be thought that what is expounded in Encyclical Letters does not of itself demand assent *(assensum)*, since the Popes do not exercise in such letters the full power of their Magisterium. For these matters are taught with the ordinary Magisterium, of which it is true to say: "He who hears you, hears me" (Lk 10:16); and generally what is expounded and inculcated in encyclical letters already for other reasons pertains to Catholic doctrine. But if the supreme pontiffs in their official documents purposely pass judgment on a matter up to that time under dispute, it is obvious that the matter, according to the mind and will of these pontiffs, cannot any longer be considered a question open to free discussion *(liberae disceptationis)* among theologians.

Vatican II in its Constitution on the Church spoke somewhat more briefly to the same point:

> Religious submission *(religiosum obsequium)* of will and intellect is to be given in a special way to the authentic Magisterium of the Roman pontiff even when he is not speaking ex cathedra; in such a way, that is, that his supreme Magisterium is respectfully acknowledged, and the judgment expressed by him is sincerely adhered to *(sincere adhaereatur)*, in accordance with his manifest mind and will, which is communicated chiefly by the nature of the documents, by the frequent repetition of the same doctrine, or by the style of verbal expression. (*LG* 25)

Lumen gentium, probably for the sake of brevity, did not repeat the statement of Pius XII regarding the termination of free discussion, but it would seem clear from its teaching on submission to the ordinary papal magisterium that theologians could not properly continue to urge their objections after the pope had rendered a contrary judgment.

Following the language of Vatican II, the Profession of Faith states that the Catholic must adhere to authentic but non-definitive teaching with "religious submission will and intellect." The term *obsequium religiosum*, introduced at this point, is notoriously difficult to translate into English. Terms such as "religious submission," "religious assent," "conditioned assent," "religious respect," "religious adherence," and "religious allegiance" have been proposed as translations. This response, like the *obsequium* of faith, is motivated by reverence for the sacred authority of the speaker, but it falls short of the absolute and irrevocable assent required in the first two categories because in this case the infallibility of the Church is not engaged. *Obsequium religiosum* can nevertheless be relatively firm in certain cases.

Because the instances of such teaching are so numerous and various, the 1998 Commentary refrained from giving examples. Such teachings, it declared, "require degrees of adherence differentiated according to the mind and will" of the teacher, as "shown especially by the nature of the document, by the frequent repetition of the same doctrine or by the tenor of the verbal expression" (§11). In an earlier instruction, *Donum veritatis* (1990), the CDF had stated that the response to such teachings "cannot be simply exterior or disciplinary, but must be understood within the logic of faith and under the impulse of obedience to the faith."[14] Nonadherence, however, is not totally excluded, for as the Instruction says a little later: "The willingness to submit loyally to the Magisterium on matters per se not irreformable must be the rule."[15] The phrasing of this sentence seems to imply that the requirements of *obsequium* can, in exceptional cases, be fulfilled by what

---

[14] Congregation for the Doctrine of the Faith, *Donum veritatis*, "Instruction on the Ecclesial Vocation of the Theologian," §23; *Origins* 20 (July 5, 1990): 117–26, at 122.

[15] Ibid., §24, 122.

Francis Sullivan calls "an honest and sustained effort to overcome any contrary opinion I might have," even when that effort does not eventuate in the actual assent of the intellect.[16]

DISCIPLINARY INTERVENTIONS

The Profession of Faith, since it is concerned only with doctrinal matters, does not deal with disciplinary interventions on the part of the Magisterium, but these are touched on in the Instruction *Donum veritatis*. Sometimes organs of the Magisterium, without pronouncing on the truth or falsity of a proposition, direct Catholic teachers and writers for pastoral reasons not to affirm it, or to affirm it only as a hypothesis until it is solidly proved. The Magisterium has exercised great caution in admitting new scientific theories that seemed contrary to Scripture and longstanding Tradition and that might be upsetting to the faithful. This was the case with regard to heliocentrism in the seventeenth century and, later, the theory of evolution. It was also true of certain responses of the Biblical Commission to theories being espoused by Modernists and critical exegetes at the beginning of the twentieth century. Disciplinary regulations of this kind are by their nature subject to change, since they reflect the state of the evidence at a particular moment of history. They require external conformity in behavior, but do not demand internal assent.

In a press conference on *Donum veritatis* Cardinal Ratzinger spoke more fully of "prudential interventions" than the text itself. He said that the anti-Modernist decisions of the Biblical Commission, even though some of them may be seen in retrospect as overrestrictive, performed a great service in saving the Church from the assaults of liberal positivism. They fulfilled a pastoral function in the situation of their day and remain valid as warnings against rash and superficial accommodations.[17]

---

[16] Sullivan, *Magisterium*, 164.

[17] Joseph Ratzinger, *The Nature and Mission of Theology* (San Francisco: Ignatius, 1995), 106.

DISSENT

To dissent means to think or assert what is contrary to the approved teaching. It occurs when one denies the truth of what is taught, or consciously affirms something that contradicts it. Dissent is sometimes confused with other responses, such as wishing that the Magisterium could have taught otherwise, or failing to understand why the Magisterium taught as it did. Dissent, however, is not the same as disappointment or incomprehension, which are entirely compatible with assent. Nor is it the same as doubt, though doubt is likewise a failure to give full assent. Depending on the circumstances, dissent or doubt may be voluntary or involuntary, culpable or inculpable. The loyal Catholic, out of respect for the Magisterium, will try to avoid dissenting from or doubting its authoritative teaching. On each of the three levels of magisterial teaching, dissent and doubt have different consequences.

1. To dissent from, or to doubt, articles of the creed and dogmas of the faith, if done obstinately, is heresy. If such dissent is expressed, the penalty of automatic excommunication is incurred. Persons who even inculpably reject what the Church definitively teaches as her faith cease to be in communion with the Church. One may have difficulties in believing certain dogmas of the faith, but difficulties do not prevent one from assenting, nor do they exclude one from communion. Those who experience serious difficulties have an obligation to try to understand the basis for the teaching, to pray over it, and to recognize that the Church is a divinely commissioned teacher. They should remind themselves that the Church is not limited to teaching what they would believe without her intervention. We most need the Church when we would fall into error unless she corrected us.

2. To dissent from definitive non-revealed teaching, or to doubt it, is not heresy. But those who dissent from such doctrines are

opposed to the Church's definitive teaching and are objectively in error. In the absence of aggravating factors, such as contempt for the Magisterium or scandal, such dissenters are not excommunicated or excluded from the sacraments, but their communion is in some ways impaired. Theologians who dissent from doctrines in this second category frequently claim that the doctrines are not definitively taught, but properly belong in added paragraph 3. But this evasion is not acceptable in cases in which the Magisterium clearly teaches that the doctrines must be definitively held.[18]

3. The problem of dissent arises most frequently in connection with added paragraph 3, which deals with teachings that might in principle be erroneous. The Church recognizes that personal difficulties with such teachings can occur, even among faithful theologians. But as the CDF states in *Donum veritatis*, the presumption should always be in favor of the Magisterium, because God has given it to the Church as a

---

[18] At the Vallombrosa meeting the representatives of the CDF stated with reference to *Ordinatio sacerdotalis*: "It would be contrary to the teaching of the Church to maintain that this doctrine belongs to the third paragraph, and as such requires only religious submission of intellect and will, and not a firm and irrevocable assent" (*Vallombrosa Papers*, 65). In an *ad limina* speech to German bishops of November 20, 1999, Pope John Paul II himself declared that "the doctrine that the priesthood is reserved to men possesses, by virtue of the Church's ordinary and universal Magisterium, that character of infallibility which *Lumen gentium* speaks of and to which I gave juridical form in the Motu Proprio *Ad tuendam fidem*."

As for the teaching of *Humanae vitae*, it is not mentioned in the Ratzinger-Bertone Commentary on the Profession of Faith. But the Pontifical Council on the Family, in its *Vademecum for Confessors concerning some Aspects of the Morality of Conjugal Life*, dated February 12, 1997, declared: "The Church has always taught the intrinsic evil of contraception, that is, of every marital act rendered unfruitful. This teaching is to be held as definitive and irreformable." If so, the sinfulness of contraception probably falls within the second added paragraph of the Profession of Faith.

guide and assists it with special graces. Even when theologians do not see the reasons for a particular teaching, they will assume that the pope and the bishops have good reasons as yet unknown to them. They will study, consult, and pray before allowing themselves to disagree.[19]

It is important, however, to recognize that magisterial interventions of the prudential order are not always free from contingent and conjectural elements that can be sifted out only with the passage of time. The effort to identify such non-essential features is an important task of theology, and should not be confused with dissent, provided that the substantive teaching is accepted.[20]

If, in an exceptional case, one feels justified in dissenting, the next question is what to do about it. One option is to remain silent, so as not to trouble other believers and cause division in the Church. It can be assumed that if the Magisterium has erred, it will correct itself. Many of the older textbooks recommended a *silentium obsequiosum* (reverent silence). *Donum veritatis* speaks of situations in which the theologian will be called "to suffer for the truth, in silence and prayer, but with the certainty that if the truth is really at stake it will ultimately prevail."[21] Today it is not uncommon to hold that dissenters who are qualified experts should make their disagreements known, with the aim of being corrected by colleagues or, alternatively, to "provide a stimulus to the Magisterium to propose the teaching of the Church in greater depth and with a clearer presentation of the arguments."[22] An expressed dissent can be private, if it is shared only with a relatively small group, or public, if shared with a wide audience. According to *Donum veritatis*, theologians who have difficulty in accepting some doctrine would

---

[19] CDF, Instruction *Donum veritatis*, §§24–31, 122–23.
[20] Ibid., §24, 122–23.
[21] Ibid., §31, 123.
[22] Ibid., §30, 123.

generally do well to enter privately into communication with a few colleagues, to see how they react, and perhaps also to make their difficulties discreetly known to hierarchical teachers, for the reasons mentioned above. The development of doctrine has sometimes been assisted by expressions of dissatisfaction with previous deficient formulations. This observation of the CDF is noteworthy, since it is relatively new for theologians to receive official encouragement to express their problems with current magisterial teaching.

The other possibility is to dissent publicly, disseminating one's views through popular media of communication. Occasionally dissenting theologians have called press conferences and taken out advertisements in secular newspapers to announce that the Magisterium is misleading the Church and to promote their own position as the preferable alternative. Public opposition of this sort is a usurpation of authority, because the dissenters claim to be correcting the divinely constituted Magisterium. The CDF particularly disapproves of organized dissent, especially when it is used to put pressure on the Magisterium to change its teaching.[23] It harms the Church in the eyes of the general public; it weakens the Church by dividing Catholics against one another; and it is usually counterproductive because it prompts the hierarchical Magisterium to stiffen its stance lest it appear to be yielding to pressure.

The line between private and public dissent is not always clear. What begins as private dissent, communicated in a restricted scholarly circle, often finds its way into the press and becomes public. If this happens in an unforeseeable way, the theologian is not responsible. But reasonable efforts should be taken to prevent the confusion, bitterness, and disrespect for authority that normally accompany public opposition.

---

[23] For discussion of the CDF position on dissent, see Avery Dulles, *The Craft of Theology*, 2d ed. (New York: Crossroad, 1995), 113–16.

Dissent has always been a problem in the Church, but it seems to have become more widespread in recent years. People who live in a free democratic society have difficulty in understanding why they ought to submit their minds to a Magisterium. They often fail to understand the distinctiveness of the Church as a community of faith. Membership in the Church, unlike membership in secular societies, depends upon sharing the beliefs of the community. Christ equipped the Church with a hierarchical Magisterium that has the competence to articulate what the members should believe to keep them united among themselves and, most importantly, united to their divine Teacher. The Magisterium should be seen not as a burden but as a gift and a blessing.

CHAPTER EIGHT

■ ■ ■

Reception

THE TERM "Magisterium" is in some ways misleading. It connotes mastery, dominion. The official teachers in the Church, however, are not masters but servants of the word. According to Vatican II, "This teaching office is not above the word of God, but serves it, teaching what has been handed on, listening to it devoutly, guarding it scrupulously, and explaining it faithfully by divine commission and with the help of the Holy Spirit" (*DV* 10). Magisterium is therefore a kind of *ministerium*, service.

FAITH AS RECEPTION

The ministerial character of the teaching office belongs to the very essence of Christianity as a message that comes from on high. Jesus said of himself, "I can do nothing on my own authority; as I hear, so I judge" (Jn 5:30). "The word that I say to you I do not speak on my own authority, but the Father who dwells in me does the works" (Jn 14:10). "The word that you hear is not mine but the Father's who sent me" (Jn 14:29). Although he spoke the words of life, his word for the most part fell on barren ground. "He came to his own home, but his own people received him not" (Jn 1:11). But to all who did receive him, he became the source of everlasting life.

When Jesus returned to the Father, he sent the Holy Spirit, who likewise speaks only what he hears. "When the Spirit of truth comes, he will guide you into all the truth; for he will not speak on his own authority, but what he hears he will speak" (Jn 16:13). After Pentecost, the Holy Spirit began to carry on his work, giving power and unction to the preaching of the Apostles and their associates.

For all Christians, faith is something that comes by hearing, and what is heard comes by the preaching of Christ (Rom 10:17). Paul himself, as an Apostle, claims only to be relaying what he has heard. In his account of the Last Supper he emphatically makes the point that he has delivered to the Corinthians only what he himself received: "For I received from the Lord what I also delivered to you" (1 Cor 11:23). Again, in passing on the Resurrection kerygma, Paul writes: "For I delivered to you as of the first importance what I also received" (1 Cor 15:3). In these texts Paul uses the terms *paradidonai* and *paralambanein*, Greek equivalents for the terms used by the rabbis to describe the process of handing on and receiving the tradition. What the Apostle proclaims is the same as that which he received.

In the New Testament and in Christian theology, reception is not merely passive submission; it is a joyful and liberating response to the good news of the Gospel, a welcoming acceptance of the Lord. The Holy Spirit is both the transcendent source and the indwelling agent of reception.

THE MAGISTERIUM AS RECEPTIVE

The bishops have responsibilities analogous to those of the Apostles, whom they succeed. Joseph Ratzinger, in a work published shortly before he became pope, put the matter well:

> The task of the teaching office is not to oppose thinking, but to ensure that the authority of the answer that was bestowed on us has its say and, thus, to make room for the truth itself to enter. To

be given such a task is exciting and dangerous. It requires the humility of submission, of listening and obeying. It is a matter not of putting your own ideas in effect, but of keeping a place for what the Other has to say, that Other without whose ever-present Word all else drops into the void. The teaching office, properly understood, must be a humble service undertaken to ensure that true theology remains possible and that the answers may thus be heard without which we cannot live aright.[1]

Since the earliest centuries the Magisterium has been heavily engaged in the process of reception. The canon of Scripture was built up in this way. First of all, the leaders of the Church accepted the sacred books of the Jews that were to become the Christian Old Testament. A little later they received as canonical and authoritative certain accounts of the words and deeds of Jesus, which became the four Gospels. They received also various writings of Paul and other early Christians to complete the New Testament.

The reception of Holy Scripture is of constitutive importance for the Church. The communion of churches depends on great part on their acceptance of the same Scriptures. Religious bodies that accept a markedly different canon, as do the Latter Day Saints and the Muslims, are considered not to belong to the same Church, or not to be Christian at all.

The Gelasian Decree "On Books to Be Received and Not Received," composed about 495, receives as foundational the prophetic and apostolic books of the Old and New Testaments; it also receives "for edification" *(ad aedificationem)* the four great councils and the works of a number of holy Fathers. On the negative side, it lists a number of apocryphal Scriptures and theological works as books that are not to be read in the Church (*DS* 350–54).

Reception in the sphere of liturgy has played a major part in the history of the Church. Devotional practices spread from

---

[1] Joseph Ratzinger, *Pilgrim Fellowship of Faith: The Church as Communion* (San Francisco: Ignatius, 2005), 37.

nation to nation because they appeal to the faithful. The emigration of Eastern clergy from the East after the rise of Islam brought many Marian feasts and doctrines (such as the Presentation of Mary and her "Dormition") to the churches of the West.

In every generation the Magisterium has the task of discerning what is to be received and what is to be rejected. Listening to the many voices of the age, the pastors seek to interpret them in the light of the gospel (*GS* 4) and judge them in the light of the word of God (*GS* 44). The pastoral leaders of the Church have special responsibility "not indeed to extinguish the Spirit, but to test all things and hold fast to that which is good (cf. 1 Thess 5:12, 19–21)" (*LG* 12).

COUNCILS AND RECEPTION

Yves Congar in an important article pointed out that the history of the early councils is in great part a story of their reception.[2] The creed of Nicaea was fully received only after fifty-six years of violent contentions. The Council of Constantinople of 381 marked an end of these quarrels. But that very council, he points out, owes its designation as ecumenical in part not to its membership (which was entirely Eastern) but solely to the reception of its creed by the Council of Chalcedon as a true expression of the faith of Nicaea. The third council, that of Ephesus (431), is considered ecumenical in part because of its reception both by the followers of Bishop Cyril of Alexandria and by the opposing party led by Bishop John of Antioch. The fourth council, that of Chalcedon in 451, received the writings of Leo the Great and two letters of Cyril as well as the creed of Constantinople. Rome accepted the Christological teaching of Chalcedon, but did not receive its teaching to the effect that Constantinople, as the "new Rome," was a patriarchal see ranking

---

[2] Yves Congar, "Reception as an Ecclesiological Reality," in *Election and Consensus in the Church*, ed. Giuseppe Alberigo and Anton Weiler, Concilium 77 (New York: Herder and Herder, 1972), 43–78, esp. 46.

immediately after Rome. Thus the formal authority of the council was not sufficient to guarantee the reception of all its decrees.

A number of early councils, such as those of Tyre (335), Sardica (343), Rimini-Seleucia (359), and the notorious "robber-council" of Ephesus (449), though called with the intention of being ecumenical, failed to meet the test of reception. Later, the Lateran Council of 649 failed to be received in the East, while the Council in Trullo of 692 was rejected in the West. Theologians of the court of Charlemagne raised difficulties about Nicaea II (787), but Rome eventually received it as ecumenical—the last council to be acknowledged as ecumenical in both the East and the West.

In the fifteenth century there were problems in the West itself about the reception of the later sessions of the Council of Constance. The Council of Basel, ecumenical in the minds of its participants, was rejected by Rome. The Council of Florence, accepted as ecumenical by the Catholic Church, failed to gain ratification by the Orthodox synods, which repudiated its Decree of Union.

NON-RECEPTION

Reception is authoritative when done by organs of the Magisterium, especially when they speak definitively. In the ancient Church, reception by the five patriarchates, and especially by Rome as the principal patriarchate, was considered essential. Once a teaching has been accepted by the supreme Magisterium, the faithful are under obligation to accept it. As stated in the Declaration *Mysterium Ecclesiae*: "However much the Sacred Magisterium avails itself of the contemplation, life, and study of the faithful, its office is not reduced merely to ratifying the assent already expressed by the latter; indeed, in the interpretation and explanation of the written or transmitted word of God, the Magisterium can anticipate and demand their assent."[3]

---

[3] Congregation for the Doctrine of the Faith, Declaration *Mysterium Ecclesiae, Origins* 3 (July 19, 1973): 97, 99–100, 110–12 at 100.

Reception by the faithful is never official, but is necessary for the efficacy of any teaching. Sometimes it happens that a given teaching or set of teachings encounters resistance. In the case of non-infallible teaching, it could be a sign that the Magisterium has erred. Alternatively, it could mean that the teaching, as currently formulated, is ill-timed, one-sided, or poorly presented. But a third possibility must always be considered: that the faithful are not sufficiently attuned to the Holy Spirit.

Even in the case of definitive teaching, development occurs through a kind of dialectic of proclamation and response. The Christology of Ephesus, for example, was not incorrect but incomplete. Lending itself to a Monophysitic reading, it needed to be balanced by the complementary affirmations that would come twenty years later from Chalcedon. The teaching of Vatican I on papal primacy, according to Cardinal Newman, could be misinterpreted in ways that overemphasized the role of the pope. If the need should arise, he speculated, a future council would be able to trim the balance of doctrine by completing it, just as Chalcedon had acted to complement the teaching of Ephesus.[4]

Vatican II in fact overcame many imbalances that had affected Catholic official teaching during the years since Trent. Some scholars believe that it not only filled in deficiencies but in some respects corrected previous non-infallible teaching on subjects such as membership in the Church, Church and state, religious freedom, ecumenism, and non-Christian religions.[5] Other scholars contend that in these areas the previous teaching was not wrong but was in need of being adapted to a changed social and religious situation. The Council, they maintain, simply made a new application of principles that had long been part of the Tradition. Each of these cases is complicated and must be carefully examined for its own sake.

---

[4] Newman, "Letter to the Duke of Norfolk," in Ryan, *Newman and Gladstone*, 172–73.

[5] For discussion of these possible "reversals," see Dionne, *The Papacy and the Church*.

Since Vatican II, several controversial doctrinal decisions have met with a very mixed, even predominantly negative, reception. The encyclical *Humanae vitae*, published by Paul VI in 1968, may serve as an example. No sooner was it published than a chorus of dissent, led by prominent theologians in Western Europe and North America, broke out. Some theologians contend that the lack of reception is evidence that the teaching must have been erroneous. But this conclusion is not obvious. The mere absence of reception does not count as evidence against a teaching unless the opposition is animated by the spirit of Christ and the gospel. Otherwise the dissent may prove only that the teaching is in conflict with the spirit of the times and what Paul would call the desires of the flesh. Cardinal Wojtyla, in a retreat preached to the papal household in 1976, recalled the contestation surrounding *Humanae vitae* and remarked:

> The inheritance of salvific truth is an extremely demanding one, fraught with difficulties. Inevitably the Church's activities, and those of the Supreme Pontiff in particular, often become a "sign of contradiction." This too shows that her mission is that of Christ, who continues to be a sign of contradiction.[6]

The Church must always be on guard against being taken in by the spirit of the age. One of the great values of the hierarchical magisterium is that it gives the Church a body of teachers who are deeply immersed in Holy Scripture and Tradition, who are trained in the ways of prayer and worship and qualified by the grace of sacramental ordination to speak in the name of Christ the Lord. The indispensable task of the Magisterium is to bear witness to the truth "in season and out of season" (2 Tim 4:2). If devout believers receive the teaching favorably, God is to be praised. But if they reject the teaching for a time, this evil must be patiently endured. A

---

6 Karol Wojtyla (Pope John Paul II), *Sign of Contradiction* (New York: Seabury, 1979), 124.

perfect harmony of minds between the hierarchical teachers and the body of the faithful is the ideal for which we should pray and labor.

RECEPTION AS INTERPRETATION

Reception plays a major role in the communication of magisterial decrees. The process is not merely mechanical, but involves an exchange among living minds. As Cardinal Newman pointed out, doctrinal pronouncements normally admit of a range of interpretations. The body of theologians (which he called the *schola theologorum*) were key players in this process.[7] Newman himself ventured theological interpretations of the Syllabus of Errors and of *Pastor aeternus* that have stood up well under later scrutiny.

It often takes several generations before a consensus is reached or before the Magisterium itself issues an authentic interpretation. For example, there was considerable doubt for some years about the precise import of the term *homoousion* ("consubstantial") as used by Nicaea. Many interpreted it in a semi-Arian sense until the Council of Constantinople in 381 upheld the strict interpretation given by Athanasius and his party.

The interpretation of Vatican II has been a source of great concern over the past generation. Some interpretations placed that council in sharp opposition to Trent, Vatican I, and popes such as Pius XII. Foreseeing the likelihood that collegiality would be misunderstood in a parliamentarian sense, Paul VI wisely insisted on appending the "Prefatory Note of Explanation" to the third chapter of *Lumen gentium*.

In 1985, on the twentieth anniversary of the conclusion of the council, Pope John Paul II summoned an extraordinary assembly of the Synod of Bishops to lay down guidelines for its correct interpretation. The synod favored a hermeneutics that emphasized the letter of the documents, the interconnection among all the council documents, and their "continuity with the great tradi-

---

[7] Newman, "Letter to the Duke of Norfolk," 191–97.

tion of the Church. . . . The Church is one and the same through-out all the councils."[8]

The interpretation of magisterial pronouncements includes the reinterpretation of earlier statements in light of later ones, leading to what some theologians have called "re-reception."[9] The Council of Trent, for example, clarified by reinterpretation certain teachings of some early Western local councils that, read in a later context, might seem to support the extreme positions of those who held that after the Fall human beings were bound to sin in every deed and were incapable of performing any naturally good acts.

In the fifth century the dogmatic declarations of Ephesus and Chalcedon on Christology created divisions with several ancient churches in the East, which used different terminology from that of the councils. In recent decades the controverted decrees have been reinterpreted in ways that make it possible for patriarchs of these separated churches to unite with Catholics in Christological declarations of faith. Pope John Paul II in his encyclical *Ut unum sint* refers to recent joint declarations with the Coptic Orthodox Patriarch, the Syrian Orthodox Patriarch of Antioch, and the Assyrian Patriarch of the East, all of whom profess the same faith as Catholics in Jesus Christ, true God and true man (*UUS* 62).

ECUMENICAL DIALOGUE AND RECEPTION

This final point opens up a very large field of investigation that lies beyond the scope of the present book: the ecumenical significance

---

[8] Extraordinary Synod of Bishops, *Final Report,* I, 5; in *Origins* 15 (December 10, 1985): 444–50, at 445–46. For commentary, see Avery Dulles, "The Extraordinary Synod of 1985," in his *The Reshaping of Catholicism* (San Francisco: Harper and Row, 1988), 184–206; reprinted from Giuseppe Alberigo et al. eds., *The Reception of Vatican II* (Washington, DC: The Catholic University of America Press, 1987), 349–63.

[9] The term "re-reception" seems to have arisen in colloquia sponsored by the Faith and Order Commission in 1969 to 1971. See *Faith and Order: Louvain 1971.* Faith and Order Paper No. 59 (Geneva: World Council of Churches, 1971), 227.

of reception and re-reception. Just as in Christian antiquity the decisions of local councils could gradually win acceptance by regional churches that had not originally participated in them, so in modern times the positions taken separately by denominational churches can gradually gain recognition from other ecclesial bodies. One of the main objectives of ecumenical dialogues is to achieve such recognition. The term "ecumenical reception" is frequently used to designate what the American Lutheran William Rusch calls "an ongoing process by which a church under the guidance of God's Spirit makes the results of a bilateral or multilateral conversation a part of its faith and life because the results are seen to be in conformity with the teachings of Christ and of the apostolic community, that is, the gospel as witnessed to in Scripture."[10]

Vatican II is unique among ecumenical councils for having spoken in positive terms about churches and ecclesial communities that were outside the Catholic communion. The Decree on Ecumenism, *Unitatis redintegratio,* exhorted Catholics to recognize their basic unity in faith with all who profess the Christian name and to be receptive to all the authentic Christian values in these other communities. In its early paragraphs the Decree "receives," so to speak, the Ecumenical Movement, designating it as an impulse of grace fostered by the Holy Spirit with the objective of achieving the fullness of visible unity desired by Christ the Lord (*UR* 1, 4).

In its statements on the Orthodox churches of the East the Decree on Ecumenism makes excellent use of the theology of reception, calling attention to sociocultural factors. "The heritage handed down by the Apostles was received in different forms and ways, so that from the very beginnings of the Church it has had a varied development in various times and places, thanks to a similar

---

[10] William G. Rusch, *Reception: An Ecumenical Opportunity* (Philadelphia: Fortress, 1988). Much of the recent literature is reviewed in Hermann J. Pottmeyer, "Ecumenical Dialogue and Reception," in *L'Intelletto cristiano: studi in onore di Mons. Giuseppe Colombo* (Milan: Edizioni Glossa, 2004), 359–78.

variety of natural gifts and conditions of life" (*UR* 14). The implication seems to be that many Orthodox traditions, though different from those of the Catholic Church, are capable of being recognized and received by her. The Decree goes on to say: "It is hardly surprising, then, if sometimes one tradition has come nearer than the other to an apt appreciation of certain aspects of a revealed mystery, or has expressed them in a clearer manner" (*UR* 17). The reader is led to infer that some of the disputed formulations on a question such as the procession of the Holy Spirit might eventually be seen as "complementary rather than conflicting" (*UR* 17).

This irenic approach has borne great fruit in dialogues since the council. I have already referred to the rereading of Chalcedon in such a way that its teaching can be accepted by non-Chalcedonian churches. Comparable developments have occurred in the West. During the years 1975–80 an intense debate took place, especially in Germany, regarding the possibility of Catholic recognition of the Lutheran Augsburg Confession. In a lecture of 1977 Joseph Ratzinger gave favorable attention to the proposal,[11] but in 1978 he rendered his judgment: "Since the notion of 'recognition' almost of necessity awakens false expectations, it should, in my opinion, be abandoned."[12] The debate did however, lead to a genuine rapprochement. In 1980 the German Catholic bishops wrote: "We are happy to discover not simply a partial consensus on some truths but rather a full accord on fundamental and central truths." Pope John Paul II quoted this statement and made it his own when he addressed a Lutheran body in Germany in Mainz on November 17, 1980.[13]

---

[11] Joseph Ratzinger, "The Ecumenical Situation—Orthodoxy, Catholicism and Protestantism," in his *Principles of Catholic Theology*, 193–203.

[12] Joseph Ratzinger, "Elucidations of the Question of 'Recognition' of the *Confessio Augustana* by the Catholic Church," ibid., 218–28, at 228.

[13] John Paul II, "Address to the Council of the Evangelical Church in Germany," November 17, 1980, in *Lutheran/Roman Catholic Discussion on the Augsburg Confession, Documents—1977–81*, ed. Harding Meyer (Geneva, Switzerland: Lutheran World Federation, 1982), 62–66, at 64.

As Pope John Paul II wrote in his encyclical on ecumenism, it is often necessary to find new formulations:

> Intolerant polemics and controversies have made incompatible assertions out of what was really the result of two different ways of looking at the same reality. Nowadays we need to find the formula which, by capturing the reality in its entirety, will enable us to move beyond partial readings and eliminate false interpretations (*UUS* 38).

In the restoration of Christian unity the Magisterium plays an important and indispensable role. It alone enables a church to make a definite public commitment to a doctrinal agreement. Without an official doctrinal authority to validate them, ecumenical accords remain at the stage of being mere proposals, always subject to discussion and debate. If there is to be a true doctrinal reconciliation, overcoming the conflicts of the past, it will have to be received and authenticated by the Magisterium.[14] The Magisterium thus plays an indispensable role in the life of all Christian communities and in the process of overcoming present divisions.

There is a normal human temptation to imagine that Christian unity can be achieved by compromise. If each party gives up some of its turf, we suppose, all may be able to stand together. But the truth of revelation is not a chip for bargaining. It is a precious trust that the Church is bound to preserve as the source of life for

---

[14] Something approaching mutual magisterial authentication occurred with the signing of the Joint Declaration on Justification in 1999 by authorities of the Lutheran and Catholic communities. But doubts exist about the doctrinal force of the ceremony on either side. From the Catholic side, it is noted that the principal signatory was the president of the Pontifical Council for Promoting Christian Unity, which has no doctrinal authority. Neither the pope nor the prefect of the CDF signed the agreement. See Christopher J. Malloy, *Engrafted into Christ: A Critique of the Joint Declaration* (New York: Peter Lang, 2005), 5; also Ansgar Santogrossi, *Vers Quelle Unité? Un oecuménisme en quête de cohérence* (Paris: Éd. Hora Decima, 2005), 45–69.

the world. The truth of God, if it is received, has a capacity for effecting unity far stronger than any natural ties. It breaks down all the natural, social, and cultural barriers by which people are ordinarily divided and makes them fellow-members of the one Body of Christ.

The Magisterium ranks among the ecclesial elements that keep the People of God in union with one another and their heavenly Lord. It cannot function except in subordination to Scripture and Tradition, and with the support of prayer and sacramental life. The pastors are no more than servants of communion. Like conductors of a choir, they must follow the score of the composer. They cannot function except when they find a responsive community, all of whose voices can blend into a harmonious chorus. As the Church, under their direction, sings the praises of the Lamb who sits upon the throne, she advances toward the eternal city in which no Magisterium will be needed, for all will see, with their own eyes, the mysteries in which they now believe.

APPENDICES

■ ■ ■ ■ ■

In the appendices the orthography and punctuation have been modified for consistency with usage in the main text of the book.

APPENDIX A

■ ■ ■

VATICAN COUNCIL I
DOGMATIC CONSTITUTION *DEI FILIUS* (1870)

Excerpt from Chapter 3
"Faith"

Wherefore, **by divine and Catholic faith all those things are to be believed**

- which are **contained** in the word of God as found in **Scripture** and **Tradition**,

- and which are proposed by the **Church** as matters to be believed as divinely revealed,

- whether by her **solemn judgment**

- or in her **ordinary and universal** Magisterium.

Translation taken from Norman P. Tanner, ed., *Decrees of the Ecumenical Councils* (Washington, DC: Georgetown University Press, 1990), format according to www.mb-soft.com/believe.

APPENDIX B

■ ■ ■

VATICAN COUNCIL I
DOGMATIC CONSTITUTION *PASTOR AETERNUS* (1870)

Excerpt from Chapter 4
"On the Infallible Teaching Authority of the Roman Pontiff"

1. That apostolic primacy which the Roman pontiff possesses as successor of Peter, the prince of the Apostles, includes also the supreme power of teaching.

    ○ This **Holy See** has always maintained this,

    ○ the constant **custom** of the Church demonstrates it, and

    ○ the ecumenical **councils**, particularly those in which East and West met in the union of faith and charity, have declared it.

    [councils]

2. So the fathers of the **Fourth Council of Constantinople**, following the footsteps of their predecessors, published this solemn profession of faith:

    ○ "The first condition of salvation is to maintain the rule of the true faith. . . . And since that saying of our lord Jesus Christ, You are Peter, and upon this rock I will

---

Translation taken from Norman P. Tanner, ed., *Decrees of the Ecumenical Councils* (Washington, DC: Georgetown University Press, 1990), format based on www.mb-soft.com/believe.

build my Church,[1] cannot fail of its effect, the words spoken are confirmed by their consequences. For in the apostolic see the Catholic religion has always been preserved unblemished, and sacred doctrine been held in honour. Since it is our earnest desire to be in no way separated from this faith and doctrine, we hope that we may deserve to remain in that one communion which the apostolic see preaches, for in it is the whole and true strength of the Christian religion."[2]

What is more, with the approval of the **Second Council of Lyons**, the Greeks made the following profession:

○ "The holy Roman church possesses the supreme and full primacy and principality over the whole Catholic Church. She truly and humbly acknowledges that she received this from the Lord himself in blessed Peter, the prince and chief of the apostles, whose successor the Roman pontiff is, together with the fullness of power. And since before all others she has the duty of defending the truth of the faith, so if any questions arise concerning the faith, it is by her judgment that they must be settled."[3]

Then there is the definition of the **Council of Florence**:

○ "The Roman pontiff is the true Vicar of Christ, the head of the whole Church and the father and teacher of all Christians; and to him was committed in blessed Peter, by our Lord Jesus Christ, the full power of tending, ruling and governing the whole Church."[4]

---

[1] Mt 16:18.

[2] From Pope Hormisdas's formula of the year 517 (*DS* 171).

[3] From Michael Palaeologus's profession of faith which was read out at the Second Council of Lyons (*DS* 466).

[4] Council of Florence, session 6 (*DS* 1307).

[Holy See]

3. To satisfy this pastoral office, our predecessors strove unwearyingly that the saving teaching of Christ should be spread among all the peoples of the world; and with equal care they made sure that it should be kept pure and uncontaminated wherever it was received.

[Custom]

4. It was for this reason that the bishops of the whole world, sometimes individually, sometimes gathered in synods, according to the long established custom of the churches and the pattern of ancient usage referred to this apostolic see those dangers especially which arose in matters concerning the faith. This was to ensure that any damage suffered by the faith should be repaired in that place above all where the faith can know no failing.[5]

[Holy See]

5. The Roman pontiffs, too, as the circumstances of the time or the state of affairs suggested,

- sometimes by
  - summoning ecumenical councils or
  - consulting the opinion of the churches scattered throughout the world, sometimes by
  - special synods, sometimes by
  - taking advantage of other useful means afforded by divine providence,
- defined as doctrines to be held those things which, by God's help, they knew to be in keeping with
  - Sacred Scripture and
  - the apostolic Traditions.

---

[5] St. Bernard, Ep. 190 (PL 182:1053).

6. For the Holy Spirit was promised to the successors of Peter

   ○ not so that they might, by his revelation, make known some new doctrine,

   ○ but that, by his assistance, they might religiously guard and faithfully expound the revelation or deposit of faith transmitted by the **Apostles**.

   Indeed, their apostolic teaching was

   ○ embraced by all the venerable **fathers** and

   ○ reverenced and followed by all the holy orthodox **doctors**,

   for they knew very well that this see of St. Peter always remains unblemished by any error, in accordance with the divine promise of our Lord and Saviour to the prince of his disciples: "I have prayed for you that your faith may not fail; and when you have turned again, strengthen your brethren."[6]

7. This gift of truth and never-failing faith was therefore divinely conferred on Peter and his successors in this see so that they might discharge their exalted office for the salvation of all, and so that the whole flock of Christ might be kept away by them from the poisonous food of error and be nourished with the sustenance of heavenly doctrine. Thus the tendency to schism is removed and the whole Church is preserved in unity, and, resting on its foundation, can stand firm against the gates of hell.

8. But since in this very age when the salutary effectiveness of the apostolic office is most especially needed, not a few are to be found who disparage its authority, we judge it absolutely necessary to affirm solemnly the prerogative which the only-begotten Son of God was pleased to attach to the supreme pastoral office.

---

6 Lk 22:32.

9. Therefore,

- faithfully adhering to the tradition received from the beginning of the Christian faith,
- to the glory of God our Saviour,
- for the exaltation of the Catholic religion and
- for the salvation of the Christian people,
- with the approval of the sacred council,
- we *teach and **define*** as a divinely revealed dogma that
  - when the Roman pontiff speaks EX CATHEDRA,
    - that is, when,
      1. **in the exercise of his office as shepherd and teacher of all Christians,**
      2. **in virtue of his supreme apostolic authority,**
      3. **he defines a doctrine concerning faith or morals to be held by the whole Church,**
  - he possesses,
    - by the divine assistance promised to him in blessed Peter,
    - that infallibility which the divine Redeemer willed his Church to enjoy in defining doctrine concerning faith or morals.
  - *Therefore*, such definitions of the Roman pontiff are of themselves, and not by the consent of the Church, irreformable.

So then, should anyone, which God forbid, have the temerity to reject this definition of ours: let him be **anathema**.

APPENDIX C

■ ■ ■

Pius XII, Encyclical *Humani generis* (1950)

Excerpt

18. Unfortunately these advocates of novelty easily pass from despising Scholastic theology to the neglect of and even contempt for the Teaching Authority *(Magisterium)* of the Church itself, which gives such authoritative approval to scholastic theology. This Teaching Authority is represented by them as a hindrance to progress and an obstacle in the way of science. Some non-Catholics consider it as an unjust restraint preventing some more qualified theologians from reforming their subject. And although this sacred Office of Teacher in matters of faith and morals must be the proximate and universal criterion of truth for all theologians, since to it has been entrusted by Christ Our Lord the whole deposit of faith—Sacred Scripture and divine Tradition—to be preserved, guarded and interpreted, still the duty that is incumbent on the faithful to flee also those errors which more or less approach heresy, and accordingly "to keep also the constitutions and decrees by which such evil opinions are proscribed and forbidden by the Holy See,"[1] is sometimes as little known as if it did not exist. What is expounded in the encyclical letters of the Roman pontiffs concerning the nature and constitution of the Church, is deliberately and habitually neglected by some with the idea of giving force to a

---

Text from Claudia Carlen, ed., *The Papal Encyclicals 1939–1958* (Wilmington, NC: McGrath, 1981), 178–79.

[1] Code of Canon Law (1917), c. 1324; cf. Vatican I, *DS* 3045.

certain vague notion which they profess to have found in the ancient Fathers, especially the Greeks. The popes, they assert, do not wish to pass judgment on what is a matter of dispute among theologians, so recourse must be had to the early sources, and the recent constitutions and decrees of the Teaching Church must be explained from the writings of the ancients.

19. Although these things seem well said, still they are not free from error. It is true that popes generally leave theologians free in those matters which are disputed in various ways by men of very high authority in this field; but history teaches that many matters that formerly were open to discussion, no longer now admit of discussion.

20. Nor must it be thought that what is expounded in encyclical letters does not of itself demand consent, since in writing such letters the popes do not exercise the supreme power of their Teaching Authority. For these matters are taught with the ordinary teaching authority, of which it is true to say: "He who heareth you, heareth me" (Lk 19:16); and generally what is expounded and inculcated in encyclical letters already for other reasons appertains to Catholic doctrine. But if the supreme pontiffs in their official documents purposely pass judgment on a matter up to that time under dispute, it is obvious that that matter, according to the mind and will of the same pontiffs, cannot be any longer considered a question open to discussion among theologians.

21. It is also true that theologians must always return to the sources of divine revelation: for it belongs to them to point out how the doctrine of the living Teaching Authority is to be found either explicitly or implicitly in the Scriptures and in Tradition.[2] Besides, each source of divinely revealed doctrine contains so many rich treasures of truth, that they can really never be exhausted. Hence it is that theology through the study of its sacred sources remains ever fresh; on the other hand, speculation which neglects a

---

[2] Pius IX, *Inter gravissimas,* 28 Oct. 1870; *Acta* 1:260.

deeper search into the deposit of faith, proves sterile, as we know from experience. But for this reason even positive theology cannot be on a par with merely historical science. For, together with the sources of positive theology God has given to His Church a living Teaching Authority to elucidate and explain what is contained in the deposit of faith only obscurely and implicitly. This deposit of faith our Divine Redeemer has given for authentic interpretation not to each of the faithful, not even to theologians, but only to the Teaching Authority of the Church. But if the Church does exercise this function of teaching, as she often has through the centuries, either in the ordinary or extraordinary way, it is clear how false is a procedure which would attempt to explain what is clear by means of what is obscure. Indeed the very opposite procedure must be used. Hence our predecessor of immortal memory, Pius IX, teaching that the most noble office of theology is to show how a doctrine defined by the Church is contained in the sources of revelation, added these words, and with very good reason: "in that sense in which it has been defined by the Church."

APPENDIX D

■ ■ ■

VATICAN COUNCIL II
DOGMATIC CONSTITUTION *LUMEN GENTIUM* (1964).

Excerpt

12. The holy People of God shares also in Christ's prophetic office. It spreads abroad a living witness to him, especially by means of a life of faith and charity and by offering to God a sacrifice of praise, the tribute of lips which give honor to his name (cf. Heb 13:15). The body of the faithful as a whole, anointed as they are by the Holy One (cf. 1 Jn 2:20, 27), cannot err in matters of belief. Thanks to a supernatural sense of the faith which characterizes the People as a whole, it manifests this unerring quality when, "from the bishops down to the last member of the laity,"[1] it shows universal agreement in matters of faith and morals.

For, by this sense of faith which is aroused and sustained by the Spirit of truth, God's People accepts not the word of men but the very word of God (cf. 1 Th 2:13). It clings without fail to the faith once delivered to the saints (cf. Jude 3), penetrates it more deeply by accurate insights, and applies it more thoroughly to life. All this it does under the lead of a sacred teaching authority, to which it loyally defers.

It is not only through the sacraments and Church ministries that the same Holy Spirit sanctifies and leads the People of God and

---

Translation in Walter M. Abbott, ed., *The Documents of Vatican II* (New York: America Press, 1966), 29-30. Unofficial footnotes omitted.

[1] Cf. Augustine, *De praed. sanct.,* 14:27 (PL 44:980).

enriches it with virtues. Allotting his gifts "to everyone according as he will" (1 Cor 12:11), he distributes special graces among the faithful of every rank. By these gifts he makes them fit and ready to undertake the various tasks or offices advantageous for the renewal and building up of the Church, according to the words of the Apostle: "The manifestation of the Spirit is given to everyone for profit" (1 Cor 12:7). These charismatic gifts, whether they be the most outstanding or the more simple and widely diffused, are to be received with thanksgiving and consolation, for they are exceedingly suitable and useful for the needs of the Church.

Still, extraordinary gifts are not to be rashly sought after, nor are the fruits of apostolic labor to be presumptuously expected from them. In any case, judgment as to their genuineness and proper use belongs to those who preside over the Church, and to whose special competence it belongs, not indeed to extinguish the Spirit, but to test all things and hold fast to that which is good (cf. 1 Th 5:12, 19–21).

APPENDIX E

■ ■ ■

Vatican Council II
Dogmatic Constitution *Lumen Gentium* (1964).

Excerpt

25. Among the principal duties of bishops the preaching of the gospel occupies an eminent place.[1] For bishops are preachers of the faith who lead new disciples to Christ. They are authentic teachers, that is, teachers endowed with the authority of Christ, who preach to the people committed to them the faith they must believe and put into practice. By the light of the Holy Spirit, they make that faith clear, bringing forth from the treasury of revelation new things and old (cf. Mt 13:52) making faith bear fruit and vigilantly warding off any errors which threaten their flock (cf. 2 Tim 4:1-4).

Bishops, teaching in communion with the Roman pontiff, are to be respected by all as witnesses to divine and Catholic truth. In matters of faith and morals, the bishops speak in the name of Christ and the faithful are to accept their teaching and adhere to it with a religious assent of soul. This religious submission of will and mind must be shown in a special way to the authentic teaching authority of the Roman pontiff, even when he is not speaking ex cathedra. That is, it must be shown in such a way that his supreme

---

Translation in Walter M. Abbott, ed., *The Documents of Vatican II* (New York: America Press, 1966), 47–50. Unofficial footnotes omitted.

[1] Cf. Council of Trent, Decree on reform, Session 5, c. 2, n. 9; and Session 24, c. 4: *Conc. Oec. Decr.,* 645, 739.

Magisterium is acknowledged with reverence, the judgments made by him are sincerely adhered to, according to his manifest mind and will. His mind and will in the matter may be known chiefly either from the character of the documents, from his frequent repetition of the same doctrine, or from his manner of speaking.

Although the individual bishops do not enjoy the prerogative of infallibility, they can nevertheless proclaim Christ's doctrine infallibly. This is so, even when they are dispersed around the world, provided that while maintaining the bond of unity among themselves and with Peter's successor, and while teaching authentically on a matter of faith or morals, they concur in a single viewpoint as the one which must be held conclusively.[2] This authority is even more clearly verified when, gathered together in an ecumenical council, they are teachers and judges of faith and morals for the universal Church. Their definitions must then be adhered to with the submission of faith.[3]

This infallibility with which the divine Redeemer willed to his Church to be endowed in defining a doctrine of faith and morals extends as far as extends the deposit of divine revelation, which must be religiously guarded and faithfully expounded. This is the infallibility which the Roman pontiff, the head of the college of bishops, enjoys in virtue of his office, when, as the supreme shepherd and teacher of all the faithful, who confirms his brethren in their faith (cf. Lk 22:32), he proclaims by a definitive act some doctrine of faith or morals.[4] Therefore his definitions, of themselves, and not from the consent of the Church, are justly styled

---

[2] Cf. Vatican Council I, the Dogmatic Constitution: *Dei Filius,* 3: *Denz.* 1712 (3011). Cf. note (taken from St. Robert Bellarmine) adjoined to Schema I *De Ecclesia:* Mansi 51, 579 C; as well as the revised Schema for the second constitution *De Ecclesia Christi* with the commentary of Kleutgen: Mansi 53, 313 AB. Cf. Pius IX, epistle *Tuas libenter*: *Denz.* 1683 (2879).

[3] Cf. Code of Canon Law, cc. 1322–23.

[4] Cf. Vatican Council I, the Dogmatic Constitution *Pastor aeternus*: *Denz.* 1839 (3074).

irreformable, for they are pronounced with the assistance of the Holy Spirit, an assistance promised to him in blessed Peter. Therefore they need no approval of others, nor do they allow an appeal to any other judgment. For then the Roman pontiff is not pronouncing judgment as a private person. Rather, as the supreme teacher of the universal Church, as one in whom the charism of infallibility of the Church herself is individually present, he is expounding or defending a doctrine of Catholic faith.[5]

The infallibility promised to the Church resides also in the body of bishops when that body exercises supreme teaching authority with the successor of Peter. To the resultant definitions the assent of the Church can never be wanting, on account of the activity of that same Holy Spirit, whereby the whole flock of Christ is preserved and progresses in unity of faith.[6]

But when either the Roman pontiff or the body of bishops together with him formulates a definition, they do so in accord with revelation itself. All are obliged to maintain and be ruled by this revelation, which, as written or preserved by Tradition, is transmitted in its entirety through the legitimate succession of bishops and especially through the care of the Roman pontiff himself.

Under the guiding light of the Spirit of truth, revelation is thus religiously preserved and faithfully expounded in the Church.[7] The Roman pontiff and the bishops, in conformity with their duty and as befits the gravity of the matter, strive painstakingly and by appropriate means to inquire properly into that revelation and to give apt expression to its contents.[8] But they do not accept any new public revelation as part of the divine deposit of faith.[9]

---

[5] Cf. explanation of Gasser at Vatican Council I: Mansi, 52, 1213 AC.

[6] Gasser, Vatican Council I: Mansi, 52, 1214 A.

[7] Gasser, Vatican Council I: Mansi, 52, 1215 CD, 1216–7 A.

[8] Gasser, Vatican Council I: Mansi, 52, 1213.

[9] Vatican Council I, the Dogmatic Constitution *Pastor aeternus*, 4: *Denz.* 1836 (3070).

APPENDIX F

■ ■ ■

CONGREGATION FOR THE DOCTRINE OF THE FAITH (1989)

Profession of Faith

(Formula to be employed henceforth in cases in which the profession of faith is required by law.)

I, N., with firm faith believe and profess each and every thing *(omnia et singula)* that is contained in the symbol of faith: namely,

I believe in one God, the Father, the Almighty, maker of heaven and earth, of all that is seen and unseen. I believe in one Lord, Jesus Christ, the only Son of God, eternally begotten of the Father, God from God, Light from Light, true God from true God, begotten, not made, one in Being with the Father. Through him all things were made. For us men and for our salvation he came down from heaven: By the power of the Holy Spirit, he was born of the Virgin Mary, and became man. For our sake he was crucified under Pontius Pilate; he suffered, died and was buried. On the third day he rose again in fulfillment of the Scriptures; he ascended into heaven and is seated at the right hand of the Father. He will come again in glory to judge the living and the dead, and his kingdom will have no end. I believe in the Holy Spirit, the Lord, the giver of life, who proceeds from the Father and the Son. With the Father and the Son he is worshipped and glorified. He has spoken through the Prophets. I believe in the one holy

Translation from *Origins* 18 (March 16, 1989): 663.

Catholic and apostolic Church. I acknowledge one baptism for the forgiveness of sins. I look for the resurrection of the dead, and the life of the world to come. Amen.

With firm faith I believe as well everything *(ea omnia)* contained in God's word, written or handed down in Tradition and proposed by the Church—whether by way of solemn judgment or in the ordinary and universal Magisterium—as divinely revealed and calling for faith *(tamquam divinitus revelata credenda).*

I also firmly accept and hold each and every thing *(omnia et singula)* that is proposed by that same Church definitively *(definitive)* with regard to teaching concerning faith or morals.

Moreover, I adhere *(adhaereo)* with religious submission of will and intellect *(religioso voluntatis et intellectus obsequio)* to the teachings which either the Roman pontiff or the college of bishops enunciate when they exercise the authentic Magisterium even if they proclaim those teachings in an act that is not definitive.

APPENDIX G

■ ■ ■

CONGREGATION FOR THE DOCTRINE OF THE FAITH INSTRUCTION ON THE ECCLESIAL VOCATION OF THE THEOLOGIAN, *DONUM VERITATIS* (1990)

Introduction

1. The truth which sets us free is a gift of Jesus Christ (cf. Jn 8:32). Man's nature calls him to seek the truth while ignorance keeps him in a condition of servitude. Indeed, man could not be truly free were no light shed upon the central questions of his existence including, in particular, where he comes from and where he is going. When God gives himself to man as a friend, man becomes free, in accordance with the Lord's word: "No longer do I call you servants, for the servant does not know what his master is doing; but I have called you friends, for all that I have heard from my Father I have made known to you" (Jn 15:15). Man's deliverance from the alienation of sin and death comes about when Christ, the Truth, becomes the "way" for him (cf. Jn 14:6).

In the Christian faith, knowledge and life, truth and existence are intrinsically connected. Assuredly, the truth given in God's revelation exceeds the capacity of human knowledge, but it is not opposed to human reason. Revelation in fact penetrates human reason, elevates it, and calls it to give an account of itself (cf. 1 Pet 3:15). For this reason, from the very beginning of the Church, the "standard of teaching" (cf. Rom 6:17) has been linked with baptism

Text taken from *Origins* 20 (July 5, 1990): 117, 119–26.

to entrance into the mystery of Christ. The service of doctrine, implying as it does the believer's search for an understanding of the faith, for example, theology, is therefore something indispensable for the Church.

Theology has importance for the Church in every age so that it can respond to the plan of God "who desires all men to be saved and to come to the knowledge of the truth" (1 Tim 2:4). In times of great spiritual and cultural change, theology is all the more important. Yet it also is exposed to risks since it must strive to "abide" in the truth (cf. Jn 8:31), while at the same time taking into account the new problems which confront the human spirit. In our century, in particular, during the periods of preparation for and implementation of the Second Vatican Council, theology contributed much to a deeper "understanding of the realities and the words handed on."[1] But it also experienced and continues to experience moments of crisis and tension.

The Congregation for the Doctrine of the Faith deems it opportune then to address to the bishops of the Catholic Church, and through them her theologians, the present instruction which seeks to shed light on the mission of theology in the Church. After having considered truth as God's gift to his people (I), the instruction will describe the role of theologians (II), ponder the particular mission of the Church's pastors (III), and finally, propose some points on the proper relationship between theologians and pastors (IV). In this way, it aims to serve the growth in understanding of the truth (cf. Col 1:10), which ushers us into that freedom which Christ died and rose to win for us (cf. Gal 5:1).

I. THE TRUTH, GOD'S GIFT TO HIS PEOPLE

2. Out of his infinite love, God desired to draw near to man, as he seeks his own proper identity, and walk with him (cf. Lk 24:15). He also wanted to free him from the snares of the "father

---

[1] *Dei Verbum*, 8.

of lies" (cf. Jn 8:44) and to open the way to intimacy with himself so that man could find there, superabundantly, full truth and authentic freedom. This plan of love, conceived by "the Father of lights" (Jas 1:17; cf. 1 Pet 2:9; 1 Jn 1:5) and realized by the Son victorious over death (cf. Jn 8:36), is continually made present by the Spirit who leads "to all truth" (Jn 16:13).

3. The truth possesses in itself a unifying force. It frees men from isolation and the oppositions in which they have been trapped by ignorance of the truth. And as it opens the way to God, it, at the same time, unites them to each other. Christ destroyed the wall of separation which had kept them strangers to God's promise and to the fellowship of the covenant (cf. Eph 2:12–14). Into the hearts of the faithful he sends his Spirit through whom we become nothing less than "one" in him (cf. Rom 5:5; Gal 3:28). Thus thanks to the new birth and the anointing of the Holy Spirit (cf. Jn 3:5; 1 Jn 2:20, 27), we become the one, new People of God whose mission it is, with our different vocations and charisms, to preserve and hand on the gift of truth. Indeed, the whole Church, as the "salt of the earth" and "the light of the world" (cf. Mt 5:13f), must bear witness to the truth of Christ which sets us free.

4. The People of God respond to this calling "above all by means of the life of faith and charity, and by offering to God a sacrifice of praise." More specifically, as far as the "life of faith" is concerned, the Second Vatican Council makes it clear that "the whole body of the faithful who have an anointing that comes from the holy one (cf. 1 Jn 2:20, 27) cannot err in matters of belief." And "this characteristic is shown in the supernatural sense of the faith of the whole people, when 'from the bishops to the last of the faithful,' they manifest a universal consent in matters of faith and morals."[2]

5. In order to exercise the prophetic function in the world, the People of God must continually reawaken or "rekindle" its own

---

[2] *Lumen gentium,* 12.

life of faith (cf. 2 Tim 1:6). It does this particularly by contemplating ever more deeply, under the guidance of the Holy Spirit, the contents of the faith itself and by dutifully presenting the reasonableness of the faith to those who ask for an account of it (cf. 1 Pet 3:15). For the sake of this mission, the Spirit of truth distributes among the faithful of every rank special graces "for the common good" (1 Cor 12:7–11).

II. THE VOCATION OF THE THEOLOGIAN

6. Among the vocations awakened in this way by the Spirit in the Church is that of the theologian. His role is to pursue in a particular way an ever deeper understanding of the word of God found in the inspired Scriptures and handed on by the living Tradition of the Church. He does this in communion with the Magisterium which has been charged with the responsibility of preserving the deposit of faith.

By its nature, faith appeals to reason because it reveals to man the truth of his destiny and the way to attain it. Revealed truth, to be sure, surpasses our telling. All our concepts fall short of its ultimately unfathomable grandeur (cf. Eph 3:19). Nonetheless, revealed truth beckons reason—God's gift fashioned for the assimilation of truth—to enter into its light and thereby come to understand in a certain measure what it has believed. Theological science responds to the invitation of truth as it seeks to understand the faith. It thereby aids the People of God in fulfilling the Apostle's command (cf. 1 Pet 3:15) to give an accounting for their hope to those who ask it.

7. The theologian's work thus responds to a dynamism found in the faith itself. Truth, by its nature, seeks to be communicated since man was created for the perception of truth and from the depths of his being desires knowledge of it so that he can discover himself in the truth and find there his salvation (cf. 1 Tim 2:4). For this reason, the Lord sent forth his Apostles to make "disciples" of all nations

and teach them (cf. Mt 28:19f). Theology, which seeks the "reasons of faith" and offers these reasons as a response to those seeking them, thus constitutes an integral part of obedience to the command of Christ, for men cannot become disciples if the truth found in the word of faith is not presented to them (cf. Rom 10:14f).

Theology therefore offers its contribution so that the faith might be communicated. Appealing to the understanding of those who do not yet know Christ, it helps them to seek and find faith. Obedient to the impulse of truth which seeks to be communicated, theology also arises from love and love's dynamism. In the act of faith, man knows God's goodness and begins to love him. Love, however, is ever desirous of a better knowledge of the beloved.[3] From this double origin of theology, inscribed upon the interior life of the People of God and its missionary vocation, derives the method with which it ought to be pursued in order to satisfy the requirements of its nature.

8. Since the object of theology is the Truth which is the living God and his plan for salvation revealed in Jesus Christ, the theologian is called to deepen his own life of faith and continuously unite his scientific research with prayer.[4] In this way, he will become more open to the "supernatural sense of faith" upon which he depends, and it will appear to him as a sure rule for guiding his reflections and helping him assess the correctness of his conclusions.

9. Through the course of centuries, theology has progressively developed into a true and proper science. The theologian must therefore be attentive to the epistemological requirements of his discipline, to the demands of rigorous critical standards, and thus

---

[3] Cf. St. Bonaventure, *Prooem. in I Sent.,* q. 2, ad 6: "quando fides non assentit propter rationem, sed propter amorem eius cui assentit, desiderat habere rationes."

[4] Cf. John Paul II, "Address at the Conferral of the First International Paul VI Prize to Hans Urs von Balthasar, June 23, 1984," *Insegnamenti di Giovanni Paolo II,* VII, 1 (1984) 1911–17.

to a rational verification of each stage of his research. The obligation to be critical, however, should not be identified with the critical spirit which is born of feeling or prejudice. The theologian must discern in himself the origin of and motivation for his critical attitude and allow his gaze to be purified by faith. The commitment to theology requires a spiritual effort to grow in virtue and holiness.

10. Even though it transcends human reason, revealed truth is in profound harmony with it. It presumes that reason by its nature is ordered to the truth in such a way that, illumined by faith, it can penetrate to the meaning of revelation. Despite the assertions of many philosophical currents, but in conformity with a correct way of thinking which finds confirmation in Scripture, human reason's ability to attain truth must be recognized as well as its metaphysical capacity to come to a knowledge of God from creation.[5]

Theology's proper task is to understand the meaning of revelation and this, therefore, requires the utilization of philosophical concepts which provide "a solid and correct understanding of man, the world, and God"[6] and can be employed in a reflection upon revealed doctrine. The historical disciplines are likewise necessary for the theologian's investigations. This is due chiefly to the historical character of revelation itself which has been communicated to us in "salvation history." Finally, a consultation of the "human sciences" is also necessary to understand better the revealed truth about man and the moral norms for his conduct, setting these in relation to the sound findings of such sciences.

It is the theologian's task in this perspective to draw from the surrounding culture those elements which will allow him better to illumine one or other aspect of the mysteries of faith. This is certainly an arduous task that has its risks, but it is legitimate in itself and should be encouraged.

---

[5] Cf. Vatican Council I, *De Fide Catholica,* De Revelatione, canon l: *DS* 3026.

[6] *Optatam totius,* 15.

Here it is important to emphasize that when theology employs the elements and conceptual tools of philosophy or other disciplines, discernment is needed. The ultimate normative principle for such discernment is revealed doctrine which itself must furnish the criteria for the evaluation of these elements and conceptual tools and not vice versa.

11. Never forgetting that he is also a member of the People of God, the theologian must foster respect for them and be committed to offering them a teaching which in no way does harm to the doctrine of the faith.

The freedom proper to theological research is exercised within the Church's faith. Thus while the theologian might often feel the urge to be daring in his work, this will not bear fruit or "edify" unless it is accompanied by that patience which permits maturation to occur. New proposals advanced for understanding the faith "are but an offering made to the whole Church. Many corrections and broadening of perspectives within the context of fraternal dialogue may be needed before the moment comes when the whole Church can accept them." Consequently, "this very disinterested service to the community of the faithful," which theology is, "entails in essence an objective discussion, a fraternal dialogue, an openness and willingness to modify one's own opinions."[7]

12. Freedom of research, which the academic community rightly holds most precious, means an openness to accepting the truth that emerges at the end of an investigation in which no element has intruded that is foreign to the methodology corresponding to the object under study.

---

[7] John Paul II, "Address to Theologians at Altötting," November 18, 1980: *AAS* 73 (1981), 104; cf. also Paul VI, "Address to the International Theological Commission," October 11, 1972: *AAS* 64 (1972): 682–83; John Paul II, "Address to the International Theological Commission," October 26, 1979: *AAS* 71 (1979), 1428–33.

In theology this freedom of inquiry is the hallmark of a rational discipline whose object is given by revelation, handed on and interpreted in the Church under the authority of the Magisterium, and received by faith. These givens have the force of principles. To eliminate them would mean to cease doing theology. In order to set forth precisely the ways in which the theologian relates to the Church's teaching authority, it is appropriate now to reflect upon the role of the Magisterium in the Church.

III. THE MAGISTERIUM OF THE CHURCH'S PASTORS

13. "God graciously arranged that the things he had once revealed for the salvation of all peoples should remain in their entirety, throughout the ages, and be transmitted to all generations."[8] He bestowed upon his Church, through the gift of the Holy Spirit, a participation in his own infallibility.[9] Thanks to the "supernatural sense of faith," the People of God enjoys this privilege under the guidance of the Church's living Magisterium, which is the sole authentic interpreter of the word of God, written or handed down, by virtue of the authority which it exercises in the name of Christ.[10]

14. As successors of the apostles, the bishops of the Church "receive from the Lord, to whom all power is given in heaven and on earth, the mission of teaching all peoples, and of preaching the Gospel to every creature, so that all men may attain to salvation."[11] They have been entrusted then with the task of preserving, explaining, and spreading the word of God of which they are servants.[12]

---

[8] *Dei Verbum*, 7.

[9] Cf. Congregation for the Doctrine of the Faith, *Mysterium Ecclesiae*, 2: *AAS* 65 (1973): 398ff.

[10] Cf. *Dei Verbum*, 10.

[11] *Lumen gentium*, 24.

[12] Cf. *Dei Verbum*, 10.

It is the mission of the Magisterium to affirm the definitive character of the covenant established by God through Christ with his People in a way which is consistent with the "eschatological" nature of the event of Jesus Christ. It must protect God's People from the danger of deviations and confusion, guaranteeing them the objective possibility of professing the authentic faith free from error, at all times and in diverse situations. It follows that the sense and the weight of the Magisterium's authority are only intelligible in relation to the truth of Christian doctrine and the preaching of the true word. The function of the Magisterium is not, then, something extrinsic to Christian truth nor is it set above the faith. It arises directly from the economy of the faith itself, inasmuch as the Magisterium is, in its service to the word of God, an institution positively willed by Christ as a constitutive element of his Church. The service to Christian truth which the Magisterium renders is thus for the benefit of the whole People of God called to enter the liberty of the truth revealed by God in Christ.

15. Jesus Christ promised the assistance of the Holy Spirit to the Church's pastors so that they could fulfill their assigned task of teaching the Gospel and authentically interpreting revelation. In particular, he bestowed on them the charism of infallibility in matters of faith and morals. This charism is manifested when the pastors propose a doctrine as contained in revelation and can be exercised in various ways. Thus it is exercised particularly when the bishops in union with their visible head proclaim a doctrine by a collegial act, as is the case in an ecumenical council, or when the Roman pontiff, fulfilling his mission as supreme pastor and teacher of all Christians, proclaims a doctrine ex cathedra.[13]

16. By its nature, the task of religiously guarding and loyally expounding the deposit of divine revelation (in all its integrity and purity), implies that the Magisterium can make a pronouncement

---

[13] Cf. *Lumen gentium*, 25; *Mysterium Ecclesiae*, 3.

"in a definitive way"[14] on propositions which, even if not contained among the truths of faith, are nonetheless intimately connected with them, in such a way, that the definitive character of such affirmations derives in the final analysis from revelation itself.[15]

What concerns morality can also be the object of the authentic Magisterium because the Gospel, being the word of life, inspires and guides the whole sphere of human behavior. The Magisterium, therefore, has the task of discerning, by means of judgments normative for the consciences of believers those acts which in themselves conform to the demands of faith and foster their expression in life and those which, on the contrary, because intrinsically evil, are incompatible with such demands. By reason of the connection between the orders of creation and redemption and by reason of the necessity, in view of salvation, of knowing and observing the whole moral law, the competence of the Magisterium also extends to that which concerns the natural law.[16]

Revelation also contains moral teachings which per se could be known by natural reason. Access to them, however, is made difficult by man's sinful condition. It is a doctrine of faith that these moral norms can be infallibly taught by the Magisterium.[17]

17. Divine assistance is also given to the successors of the Apostles teaching in communion with the successor of Peter, and in a particular way, to the Roman pontiff as pastor of the whole Church, when exercising their ordinary Magisterium, even should this not issue in an infallible definition or in a "definitive" pronouncement but in the proposal of some teaching which leads to a better

---

[14] Cf. Profession of faith and oath of Fidelity: *AAS* 81 (1989) 104f: *"omnia et singula quae circa doctrinam de fide vel moribus ab eadem definitive proponuntur."*

[15] Cf. *Lumen gentium*, 25; *Mysterium Ecclesiae*, 3–5, 400–4; Profession of faith and oath of fidelity: *AAS* 81 (1989): 104f.

[16] Cf. Paul VI, *Humanae vitae*, 4: *AAS* 60 (1968): 483.

[17] Cf. Vatican Council, I, *Dei Filius*, ch. 2: *DS* 3005.

understanding of revelation in matters of faith and morals and to moral directives derived from such teaching.

One must therefore take into account the proper character of every exercise of the Magisterium, considering the extent to which its authority is engaged. It is also to be borne in mind that all acts of the Magisterium derive from the same source, that is, from Christ who desires that his People walk in the entire truth. For this same reason, magisterial decisions in matters of discipline, even if they are not guaranteed by the charism of infallibility, are not without divine assistance and call for the adherence of the faithful.

18. The Roman pontiff fulfills his universal mission with the help of the various bodies of the Roman Curia and in particular with that of the Congregation for the Doctrine of the Faith in matters of doctrine and morals. Consequently, the documents issued by this Congregation expressly approved by the pope participate in the ordinary Magisterium of the successor of Peter.[18]

19. Within the particular Churches, it is the bishop's responsibility to guard and interpret the word of God and to make authoritative judgments as to what is or is not in conformity with it. The teaching of each bishop, taken individually, is exercised in communion with the Roman pontiff, pastor of the universal Church, and with the other bishops dispersed throughout the world or gathered in an ecumenical council. Such communion is a condition for its authenticity.

Member of the Episcopal College by virtue of his sacramental ordination and hierarchical communion, the bishop represents his church just as all the bishops, in union with the pope, represent the Church universal in the bonds of peace, love, unity, and truth. As they come together in unity, the local churches, with their own proper patrimonies, manifest the Church's catholicity. The episcopal

---

[18] Cf. Code of Canon Law, cann. 360–61; Paul VI, *Regimini Ecclesiae Universae*, 29–40, August 15, 1967, *AAS* 59 (1967), 879–99; John Paul II, *Pastor bonus*, June 28, 1988: *AAS* 80 (1988), 873–74.

conferences for their part contribute to the concrete realization of the collegial spirit *(affectus)*.[19]

20. The pastoral task of the Magisterium is one of vigilance. It seeks to ensure that the People of God remain in the truth which sets free. It is therefore a complex and diversified reality. The theologian, to be faithful to his role of service to the truth, must take into account the proper mission of the Magisterium and collaborate with it. How should this collaboration be understood? How is it put into practice and what are the obstacles it may face? These questions should now be examined more closely.

IV. THE MAGISTERIUM AND THEOLOGY

A. Collaborative Relations

21. The living Magisterium of the Church and theology, while having different gifts and functions, ultimately have the same goal: preserving the People of God in the truth which sets free and thereby making them "a light to the nations." This service to the ecclesial community brings the theologian and the Magisterium into a reciprocal relationship. The latter authentically teaches the doctrine of the Apostles. And, benefiting from the work of theologians, it refutes objections to and distortions of the faith and promotes, with the authority received from Jesus Christ, new and deeper comprehension, clarification, and application of revealed doctrine. Theology, for its part, gains, by way of reflection, an ever deeper understanding of the word of God found in the Scripture and handed on faithfully by the Church's living Tradition under the guidance of the Magisterium. Theology strives

---

[19] *Lumen gentium,* 22–23. As it is known, following upon the second extraordinary Synod of Bishops, the Holy Father gave the Congregation for Bishops the task of exploring the "theological-juridical status of episcopal conferences."

to clarify the teaching of revelation with regard to reason and gives it finally an organic and systematic form.[20]

22. Collaboration between the theologian and the Magisterium occurs in a special way when the theologian receives the canonical mission or the mandate to teach. In a certain sense, such collaboration becomes a participation in the work of the Magisterium, linked, as it then is, by a juridic bond. The theologian's code of conduct, which obviously has its origin in the service of the word of God, is here reinforced by the commitment the theologian assumes in accepting his office, making the profession of faith, and taking the oath of fidelity.[21]

From this moment on, the theologian is officially charged with the task of presenting and illustrating the doctrine of the faith in its integrity and with full accuracy.

23. When the Magisterium of the Church makes an infallible pronouncement and solemnly declares that a teaching is found in revelation, the assent called for is that of theological faith. This kind of adherence is to be given even to the teaching of the ordinary and universal Magisterium when it proposes for belief a teaching of faith as divinely revealed.

When the Magisterium proposes "in a definitive way" truths concerning faith and morals, which, even if not divinely revealed, are nevertheless strictly and intimately connected with revelation, these must be firmly accepted and held.[22]

When the Magisterium, not intending to act "definitively," teaches a doctrine to aid a better understanding of revelation and make explicit its contents, or to recall how some teaching is in

---

20 Cf. Paul VI, "Address to International Congress on the Theology of Vatican II," October 1, 1966: *Insegnamenti di Paolo VI: AAS* 58 (1966), 892ff.

21 Cf. Canon 833; *Profession of faith and oath of fidelity.*

22 The text of the new profession of faith (cf. 15) makes explicit the kind of assent called for by these teachings in these terms: *"Firmiter etiam amplector et retineo."*

conformity with the truths of faith, or finally to guard against ideas that are incompatible with these truths, the response called for is that of the religious submission of will and intellect.[23] This kind of response cannot be simply exterior or disciplinary but must be understood within the logic of faith and under the impulse of obedience to the faith.

24. Finally, in order to serve the People of God as well as possible, in particular, by warning them of dangerous opinions which could lead to error, the Magisterium can intervene in questions under discussion which involve, in addition to solid principles, certain contingent and conjectural elements. It often only becomes possible with the passage of time to distinguish between what is necessary and what is contingent.

The willingness to submit loyally to the teaching of the Magisterium on matters per se not irreformable must be the rule. It can happen, however, that a theologian may, according to the case, raise questions regarding the timeliness, the form, or even the contents of magisterial interventions. Here the theologian will need, first of all, to assess accurately the authoritativeness of the interventions which becomes clear from the nature of the documents, the insistence with which a teaching is repeated, and the very way in which it is expressed.[24]

When it comes to the question of interventions in the prudential order, it could happen that some magisterial documents might not be free from all deficiencies. Bishops and their advisors have not always taken into immediate consideration every aspect or the entire complexity of a question. But it would be contrary to the truth, if, proceeding from some particular cases, one were to conclude that the Church's Magisterium can be habitually mistaken in its prudential judgments, or that it does not enjoy divine assistance in the integral exercise of its mission. In fact, the theologian, who

---

[23] Cf. *Lumen gentium*, 25; CIC, can. 752.
[24] *Lumen gentium*, 25:1.

cannot pursue his discipline well without a certain competence in history, is aware of the filtering which occurs with the passage of time. This is not to be understood in the sense of a relativization of the tenets of the faith. The theologian knows that some judgments of the Magisterium could be justified at the time in which they were made, because while the pronouncements contained true assertions and others which were not sure, both types were inextricably connected. Only time has permitted discernment and, after deeper study, the attainment of true doctrinal progress.

25. Even when collaboration takes place under the best conditions, the possibility cannot be excluded that tensions may arise between the theologian and the Magisterium. The meaning attributed to such tensions and the spirit with which they are faced are not matters of indifference. If tensions do not spring from hostile and contrary feelings, they can become a dynamic factor, a stimulus to both the Magisterium and theologians to fulfill their respective roles while practicing dialogue.

26. In the dialogue, a two-fold rule should prevail. When there is a question of the communion of faith, the principle of the "unity of truth" *(unitas veritatis)* applies. When it is a question of differences which do not jeopardize this communion, the "unity of charity" *(unitas caritatis)* should be safeguarded.

27. Even if the doctrine of the faith is not in question, the theologian will not present his own opinions or divergent hypotheses as though they were non-arguable conclusions. Respect for the truth as well as for the People of God requires this discretion (cf. Rom 14:1–15; 1 Cor 8; 10: 23–33). For the same reasons, the theologian will refrain from giving untimely public expression to them.

28. The preceding considerations have a particular application to the case of the theologian who might have serious difficulties, for reasons which appear to him well-founded, in accepting a non-irreformable magisterial teaching.

Such a disagreement could not be justified if it were based solely upon the fact that the validity of the given teaching is not evident or upon the opinion that the opposite position would be the more probable. Nor, furthermore, would the judgment of the subjective conscience of the theologian justify it because conscience does not constitute an autonomous and exclusive authority for deciding the truth of a doctrine.

29. In any case there should never be a diminishment of that fundamental openness loyally to accept the teaching of the Magisterium as is fitting for every believer by reason of the obedience of faith. The theologian will strive then to understand this teaching in its contents, arguments, and purposes. This will mean an intense and patient reflection on his part and a readiness, if need be, to revise his own opinions and examine the objections which his colleagues might offer him.

30. If, despite a loyal effort on the theologian's part, the difficulties persist, the theologian has the duty to make known to the magisterial authorities the problems raised by the teaching in itself, in the arguments proposed to justify it, or even in the manner in which it is presented. He should do this in an evangelical spirit and with a profound desire to resolve the difficulties. His objections could then contribute to real progress and provide a stimulus to the Magisterium to propose the teaching of the Church in greater depth and with a clearer presentation of the arguments.

In cases like these, the theologian should avoid turning to the "mass media," but have recourse to the responsible authority, for it is not by seeking to exert the pressure of public opinion that one contributes to the clarification of doctrinal issues and renders service to the truth.

31. It can also happen that at the conclusion of a serious study, undertaken with the desire to heed the Magisterium's teaching without hesitation, the theologian's difficulty remains because the

arguments to the contrary seem more persuasive to him. Faced with a proposition to which he feels he cannot give his intellectual assent, the theologian nevertheless has the duty to remain open to a deeper examination of the question.

For a loyal spirit, animated by love for the Church, such a situation can certainly prove a difficult trial. It can be a call to suffer for the truth, in silence and prayer, but with the certainty, that if the truth really is at stake, it will ultimately prevail.

B. The Problem of Dissent

32. The Magisterium has drawn attention several times to the serious harm done to the community of the Church by attitudes of general opposition to Church teaching which even come to expression in organized groups. In his Apostolic Exhortation *Paterna cum benevolentia*, Paul VI offered a diagnosis of this problem which is still apropos.[25] In particular, he addresses here that public opposition to the Magisterium of the Church also called *dissent*, which must be distinguished from the situation of personal difficulties treated above. The phenomenon of dissent can have diverse forms. Its remote and proximate causes are multiple.

The ideology of philosophical liberalism, which permeates the thinking of our age, must be counted among the factors which may exercise their remote or indirect influence. Here arises the tendency to regard a judgment as having all the more validity to the extent that it proceeds from the individual relying upon his own powers. In such a way freedom of thought comes to oppose the authority of Tradition which is considered a cause of servitude. A teaching handed on and generally received is a priori suspect and its truth contested. Ultimately, freedom of judgment understood in this way is more important than the truth itself. We are dealing then here with something quite different from the

---

25 Cf. Paul VI, *Paterna cum benevolentia*, December 8, 1974: *AAS* 67 (1975), 5–23, also *Mysterium Ecclesiae*: *AAS* 65 (1973), 396–408.

legitimate demand for freedom in the sense of absence of constraint as a necessary condition for the loyal inquiry into truth. In virtue of this exigency, the Church has always held that "nobody is to be forced to embrace the faith against his will."[26]

The weight of public opinion when manipulated and its pressure to conform also have their influence. Often models of society promoted by the "mass media" tend to assume a normative value. The view is particularly promoted that the Church should only express her judgment on those issues which public opinion considers important and then only by way of agreeing with it. The Magisterium, for example, could intervene in economic or social questions but ought to leave matters of conjugal and family morality to individual judgment.

Finally, the plurality of cultures and languages, in itself a benefit, can indirectly bring on misunderstandings which occasion disagreements.

In this context, the theologian needs to make a critical, well-considered discernment, as well as have a true mastery of the issues, if he wants to fulfill his ecclesial mission and not lose, by conforming himself to this present world (cf. Rom 12:2; Eph 4:23), the independence of judgment which should be that of the disciples of Christ.

33. Dissent has different aspects. In its most radical form, it aims at changing the Church following a model of protest which takes its inspiration from political society. More frequently, it is asserted that the theologian is not bound to adhere to any magisterial teaching unless it is infallible. Thus a kind of theological positivism is adopted, according to which, doctrines proposed without exercise of the charism of infallibility are said to have no obligatory character about them, leaving the individual completely at liberty to adhere to them or not. The theologian would accordingly be totally free to raise doubts or reject the non-infallible

---

[26] *Dignitatis humanae*, 10.

teaching of the Magisterium particularly in the case of specific moral norms. With such critical opposition, he would even be making a contribution to the development of doctrine.

34. Dissent is generally defended by various arguments, two of which are more basic in character. The first lies in the order of hermeneutics. The documents of the Magisterium, it is said, reflect nothing more than a debatable theology. The second takes theological pluralism sometimes to the point of a relativism which calls the integrity of the faith into question. Here the interventions of the Magisterium would have their origin in one theology among many theologies, while no particular theology, however, could presume to claim universal normative status. In opposition to and in competition with the authentic Magisterium, there thus arises a kind of "parallel magisterium" of theologians.[27]

Certainly, it is one of the theologian's tasks to give a correct interpretation to the texts of the Magisterium and to this end he employs various hermeneutical rules. Among these is the principle which affirms that magisterial teaching, by virtue of divine assistance, has a validity beyond its argumentation, which may derive at times from a particular theology. As far as theological pluralism is concerned, this is only legitimate to the extent that the unity of the faith in its objective meaning is not jeopardized.[28] Essential bonds link the distinct levels of unity of faith, unity-plurality of expressions of the faith, and plurality of theologies. The ultimate reason for plurality is found in the unfathomable mystery of Christ who transcends every

---

[27] The notion of a "parallel magisterium" of theologians in opposition to and in competition with the Magisterium of the pastors is sometimes supported by reference to some texts in which St. Thomas Aquinas makes a distinction between the *"magisterium cathedrae pastoralis"* and *"magisterium cathedrae magisterialis"* (*Contra impugnantes,* c. 2; *Quodlib.* III, q. 4, a.l (9); *In IV. Sent.* 19, 2, 2, q. 3 sol. 2 ad 4). Actually, these texts do not give any support to this position for St. Thomas was absolutely certain that the right to judge in matters of doctrine was the sole responsibility of the *"officium Praelationis."*

[28] *Paterna cum benevolentia,* 4.

objective systematization. This cannot mean that it is possible to accept conclusions contrary to that mystery and it certainly does not put into question the truth of those assertions by which the Magisterium has declared itself.[29] As to the "parallel magisterium," it can cause great spiritual harm by opposing itself to the Magisterium of the pastors. Indeed, when dissent succeeds in extending its influence to the point of shaping a common opinion, it tends to become the rule of conduct. This cannot but seriously trouble the People of God and lead to contempt for true authority.[30]

35. Dissent sometimes also appeals to a kind of sociological argumentation which holds that the opinion of a large number of Christians would be a direct and adequate expression of the "supernatural sense of the faith."

Actually, the opinions of the faithful cannot be purely and simply identified with the *"sensus fidei."*[31] The sense of the faith is a property of theological faith; and, as God's gift which enables one to adhere personally to the truth, it cannot err. This personal faith is also the faith of the Church since God has given guardianship of the word to the Church. Consequently, what the believer believes is what the Church believes. The *"sensus fidei"* implies then by its nature a profound agreement of spirit and heart with the Church, *"sentire cum Ecclesia."*

Although theological faith as such then cannot err, the believer can still have erroneous opinions since all his thoughts do not

---

[29] Cf. Paul VI, "Address to International Theological Commission," October 11, 1973: *AAS* 65 (1973) 555–59.

[30] Cf. John Paul II, *Redemptor hominis,* 19; "Address to the Faithful of Managua" March 4, 1983: *AAS* 75 (1983), 723; "Address to the Religious of Guatemala", 3, March 8, 1983: *AAS* 75, 746; "Address to the Bishops at Lima", 5, February 2, 1985: *AAS* 77 (1985), 874; "Address to the Bishops at Malines", 5, May 18, 1985: *Insegnamenti di Giovanni Paolo II,* VIII, 1 (1985), 1481; "Address to Some American Bishops on ad Limina Visits", 6, October 15, 1988: *L'Osservatore Romano,* October 16, 1988. p. 4.

[31] Cf. John Paul. II, *Familiaris consortio,* 5: *AAS* 74 (1982), 85–86.

spring from faith.[32] Not all the ideas which circulate among the People of God are compatible with the faith. This is all the more so given that people can be swayed by a public opinion influenced by modern communications media. Not without reason did the Second Vatican Council emphasize the indissoluble bond between the *"sensus fidei"* and the guidance of God's People by the Magisterium of the pastors. These two realities cannot be separated.[33] Magisterial interventions serve to guarantee the Church's unity in the truth of the Lord. They aid her to "abide in the truth" in face of the arbitrary character of changeable opinions and are an expression of obedience to the word of God.[34] Even when it might seem that they limit the freedom of theologians, these actions, by their fidelity to the faith which has been handed on, establish a deeper freedom which can only come from unity in truth.

36. The freedom of the act of faith cannot justify a right to dissent. In fact this freedom does not indicate at all freedom with regard to the truth but signifies the free self-determination of the person in conformity with his moral obligation to accept the truth. The act of faith is a voluntary act because man, saved by Christ the Redeemer and called by him to be an adopted son (cf. Rom 8:15; Gal 4:5; Eph 1:5; Jn 1:12), cannot adhere to God unless, "drawn by the Father" (Jn 6:44), he offers God the rational homage of his faith (cf. Rom 12:1). As the Declaration *Dignitatis humanae* recalls,[35] no human authority may overstep the limits of its competence and claim the right to interfere with

---

32 Cf. the formula of the Council of Trent, Sess. VI, Cap. 9: fides *"cui non potest subesse falsum"*: *DS* 1534; cf. St. Thomas Aquinas, *Summa theologiae* II–II, q. 1, a. 3, ad 3: *"Possibile est enim hominem fidelem ex coniectura humana falsum aliquid aestimare. Sed quod ex fide falsum aestimet, hoc est impossibile".*

33 Cf. *Lumen gentium*, 12.

34 Cf. *Dei Verbum*, 10.

35 *Dignitatis humanae*, 9–10.

this choice by exerting pressure or constraint. Respect for religious liberty is the foundation of respect for all the rights of man.

One cannot then appeal to these rights of man in order to oppose the interventions of the Magisterium. Such behavior fails to recognize the nature and mission of the Church which has received from the Lord the task to proclaim the truth of salvation to all men. She fulfills this task by walking in Christ's footsteps, knowing that "truth can impose itself on the mind only by virtue of its own truth, which wins over the mind with both gentleness and power."[36]

37. By virtue of the divine mandate given to it in the Church, the Magisterium has the mission to set forth the Gospel's teaching, guard its integrity, and thereby protect the faith of the People of God. In order to fulfill this duty, it can at times be led to take serious measures as, for example, when it withdraws from a theologian, who departs from the doctrine of the faith, the canonical mission or the teaching mandate it had given him, or declares that some writings do not conform to this doctrine. When it acts in such ways, the Magisterium seeks to be faithful to its mission of defending the right of the People of God to receive the message of the Church in its purity and integrity and not be disturbed by a particular dangerous opinion.

The judgment expressed by the Magisterium in such circumstances is the result of a thorough investigation conducted according to established procedures which afford the interested party the opportunity to clear up possible misunderstandings of his thought. This judgment, however, does not concern the person of the theologian but the intellectual positions which he has publicly espoused. The fact that these procedures can be improved does not mean that they are contrary to justice and right. To speak in this instance of a violation of human rights is out of place for it indicates a failure to recognize the proper hierarchy of these rights as well as the nature of the ecclesial community and her common good. Moreover, the the-

---

[36] Ibid., 1.

ologian who is not disposed to think with the Church *(sentire cum Ecclesia)* contradicts the commitment he freely and knowingly accepted to teach in the name of the Church.[37]

38. Finally, argumentation appealing to the obligation to follow one's own conscience cannot legitimate dissent. This is true, first of all, because conscience illumines the practical judgment about a decision to make, while here we are concerned with the truth of a doctrinal pronouncement. This is furthermore the case because while the theologian, like every believer, must follow his conscience, he is also obliged to form it. Conscience is not an independent and infallible faculty. It is an act of moral judgment regarding a responsible choice. A right conscience is one duly illumined by faith and by the objective moral law and it presupposes, as well, the uprightness of the will in the pursuit of the true good.

The right conscience of the Catholic theologian presumes not only faith in the word of God whose riches he must explore, but also love for the Church from whom he receives his mission, and respect for her divinely assisted Magisterium. Setting up a supreme magisterium of conscience in opposition to the Magisterium of the Church means adopting a principle of free examination incompatible with the economy of revelation and its transmission in the Church and thus also with a correct understanding of theology and the role of the theologian. The propositions of faith are not the product of mere individual research and free criticism of the word of God but constitute an ecclesial heritage. If there occur a separation from the bishops who watch over and keep the apostolic Tradition alive, it is the bond with Christ which is irreparably compromised.[38]

39. The Church, which has her origin in the unity of the Father, Son, and Holy Spirit,[39] is a mystery of communion. In accordance

---

[37] Cf. John Paul II, *Sapientia christiana*, 27, April 15, 1979: *AAS* 71 (1979), 483 can. 812.

[38] Cf. *Paterna cum benevolentia*, 4.

[39] Cf. *Lumen gentium*, 4.

with the will of her founder, she is organized around a hierarchy established for the service of the Gospel and the People of God who live by it. After the pattern of the members of the first community, all the baptized with their own proper charisms are to strive with sincere hearts for a harmonious unity in doctrine, life, and worship (cf. Acts 2:42). This is a rule which flows from the very being of the Church. For this reason, standards of conduct, appropriate to civil society or the workings of a democracy, cannot be purely and simply applied to the Church. Even less can relationships within the Church be inspired by the mentality of the world around it (cf. Rom 12:2). Polling public opinion to determine the proper thing to think or do, opposing the Magisterium by exerting the pressure of public opinion, making the excuse of a "consensus" among theologians, maintaining that the theologian is the prophetical spokesman of a "base" or autonomous community which would be the source of all truth, all this indicates a grave loss of the sense of truth and of the sense of the Church.

40. The Church "is like a sacrament, a sign and instrument, that is, of communion with God and of unity among all men."[40] Consequently, to pursue concord and communion is to enhance the force of her witness and credibility. To succumb to the temptation of dissent, on the other hand, is to allow the "leaven of infidelity to the Holy Spirit" to start to work.[41]

To be sure, theology and the Magisterium are of diverse natures and missions and cannot be confused. Nonetheless they fulfill two vital roles in the Church which must interpenetrate and enrich each other for the service of the People of God.

It is the duty of the pastors by virtue of the authority they have received from Christ himself to guard this unity and to see that the tensions arising from life do not degenerate into divisions. Their authority, which transcends particular positions and oppo-

---

[40] Ibid., 1.
[41] Cf. *Paterna cum benevolentia*, 2–3.

sitions, must unite all in the integrity of the Gospel which is the "word of reconciliation" (cf. 2 Cor 5:18–20).

As for theologians, by virtue of their own proper charisms, they have the responsibility of participating in the building up of Christ's Body in unity and truth. Their contribution is needed more than ever, for evangelization on a world scale requires the efforts of the whole People of God.[42] If it happens that they encounter difficulties due to the character of their research, they should seek their solution in trustful dialogue with the pastors, in the spirit of truth and charity which is that of the communion of the Church.

41. Both bishops and theologians will keep in mind that Christ is the definitive word of the Father (cf. Heb 1:2) in whom, as St. John of the Cross observes: "God has told us everything all together and at one time."[43] As such, he is the truth who sets us free (cf. Jn 8:36; 14:6). The acts of assent and submission to the word entrusted to the Church under the guidance of the Magisterium are directed ultimately to him and lead us into the realm of true freedom.

CONCLUSION

42. The Virgin Mary is Mother and perfect Icon of the Church. From the very beginnings of the New Testament, she has been called blessed because of her immediate and unhesitating assent of faith to the word of God (cf. Lk 1:38, 45), which she kept and pondered in her heart (cf. Lk 2:19, 51). Thus did she become a model and source of help for all of the People of God entrusted to her maternal care. She shows us the way to accept and serve the word. At the same time, she points out the final goal, on which our sights should ever be set, the salvation won for the world by her Son Jesus Christ which we are to proclaim to all men.

---

[42] Cf. John Paul II, *Christifideles laici*, 32–35: *AAS* 81 (1989), 451–59.

[43] St. John of the Cross, *Ascent of Mount Carmel*, II, 22, 3.

At the close of this instruction, the Congregation for the Doctrine of the Faith earnestly invites bishops to maintain and develop relations of trust with theologians in the fellowship of charity and in the realization that they share one spirit in their acceptance and service of the word. In this context, they will more easily overcome some of the obstacles which are part of the human condition on earth. In this way, all can become ever better servants of the word and of the People of God, so that the People of God, persevering in the doctrine of truth and freedom heard from the beginning, may abide also in the Son and the Father and obtain eternal life, the fulfillment of the Promise (cf. 1 Jn 2:24–25).

This instruction was adopted at an ordinary meeting of the Congregation for the Doctrine of the Faith and was approved at an audience granted to the undersigned Cardinal Prefect by the supreme pontiff, Pope John Paul II, who ordered its publication.

Given at Rome, at the Congregation for the Doctrine of the Faith, on May 24, 1990, the Solemnity of the Ascension of the Lord.

Joseph Cardinal Ratzinger   Archbishop Alberto Bovone
Prefect   *Secretary*

APPENDIX H

■ ■ ■

COMMENTARY ON THE PROFESSION OF FAITH'S CONCLUDING PARAGRAPHS, *PROFESSIO FIDEI* (1998)

1. From her very beginning, the Church has professed faith in the Lord, crucified and risen, and has gathered the fundamental contents of her belief into certain formulas. The central event of the death and resurrection of the Lord Jesus, expressed first in simple formulas and subsequently in formulas that were more developed,[1] made it possible to give life to that uninterrupted proclamation of faith in which the Church has handed on both what had been received from the lips of Christ and from his works, as well as what had been learned "at the prompting of the Holy Spirit."[2]

The same New Testament is the singular witness of the first profession proclaimed by the disciples immediately after the events of Easter: "For I handed on to you as of first importance

---

Translation from *Origins* 28 (July 16, 1998): 116–19.

[1] The simple formulas normally profess the messianic fulfillment in Jesus of Nazareth; cf. for example, Mk 8:29; Mt 16:16; Lk 9:20; Jn 20:31; Acts 9:22. The complex formulas, in addition to the resurrection, confess the principal events of the life of Jesus and their salvific meaning; cf. for example, Mk 12:35-36; Acts 2:23-24; 1 Cor 15:3-5; 1 Cor 16:22; Phil 2:7, 10-11; Col 1:15-20; 1 Pt 3:19-22; Rev 22:20. Besides the formulas of confession of faith relating to salvation history and to the historical event of Jesus of Nazareth, which culminates with Easter, there are professions of faith in the New Testament which concern the very being of Jesus: cf. 1 Cor 12:3: "Jesus is Lord." In Rom 10:9, the two forms of confession are found together.

[2] Cf. Vatican II, *Dei Verbum, 7.*

what I also received: that Christ died for our sins in accordance with the Scriptures; that he was buried; that he was raised on the third day in accordance with the Scriptures; that he appeared to Cephas, then to the Twelve."[3]

2. In the course of the centuries, from this unchangeable nucleus testifying to Jesus as Son of God and as Lord, symbols witnessing to the unity of the faith and to the communion of the churches came to be developed. In these the fundamental truths which every believer is required to know and to profess were gathered together. Thus, before receiving Baptism, the catechumen must make his profession of faith. The fathers too, coming together in councils to respond to historical challenges that required a more complete presentation of the truths of the faith or a defense of the orthodoxy of those truths, formulated new creeds which occupy "a special place in the Church's life"[4] up to the present day. The diversity of these symbols expresses the richness of the one faith; none of them is superseded or nullified by subsequent professions of faith formulated in response to later historical circumstances.

3. Christ's promise to bestow the Holy Spirit, who "will guide you into all truth," constantly sustains the Church on her way.[5] Thus in the course of her history, certain truths have been defined as having been acquired through the Holy Spirit's assistance and are therefore perceptible stages in the realization of the original promise. Other truths, however, have to be understood still more deeply before full possession can be attained of what God, in his mystery of love, wished to reveal to men for their salvation.[6]

In recent times too in her pastoral care for souls, the Church has thought it opportune to express in a more explicit way the faith of all time. In addition, the obligation has been established

---

[3] 1 Cor 15:3-5.
[4] *CCC*, 193.
[5] Jn 16:13.
[6] Cf. *Dei Verbum*, 11.

for some members of the Christian faithful, called to assume particular offices in the community in the name of the Church, to publicly make a profession of faith according to the formula approved by the Apostolic See.[7]

4. This new formula of the *Professio fidei* restates the Nicene-Constantinopolitan Creed and concludes with the addition of three propositions or paragraphs intended to better distinguish the order of the truths to which the believer adheres. The correct explanation of these paragraphs deserves a clear presentation, so that their authentic meaning, as given by the Church's Magisterium, will be well-understood, received, and integrally preserved.

In contemporary usage, the term Church has come to include a variety of meanings, which, while true and consistent, require greater precision when one refers to the specific and proper functions of persons who act within the Church. In this area, it is clear that on questions of faith and morals the only subject qualified to fulfill the office of teaching with binding authority for the faithful is the supreme pontiff and the college of bishops in communion with him.[8] The bishops are the "authentic teachers" of the faith, "endowed with the authority of Christ,"[9] because by divine institution they are the successors of the Apostles "in teaching and in pastoral governance": Together with the Roman pontiff they exercise supreme and full power over all the Church, although this power cannot be exercised without the consent of the Roman pontiff.[10]

5. The first paragraph states: "With firm faith, I also believe everything contained in the word of God, whether written or handed down in Tradition, which the Church, either by a solemn judgment or by the ordinary and universal Magisterium, sets forth to be

---

[7] Cf. Congregation for the Doctrine of the Faith, *"Profession of Faith and Oath of Fidelity": AAS* 81 (1989), 104-6; CIC, can. 833.

[8] Cf. Vatican II, *Lumen gentium,* 25.

[9] Ibid., 25.

[10] Cf. Ibid., 22.

believed as divinely revealed." The object taught in this paragraph is constituted by all those doctrines of divine and Catholic faith which the Church proposes as divinely and formally revealed and, as such, as irreformable.[11]

These doctrines *are contained in the word of God, written or handed down, and defined with a solemn judgment as divinely revealed truths either by the Roman pontiff when he speaks ex cathedra or by the college of bishops gathered in council, or infallibly proposed for belief by the ordinary and universal Magisterium.*

These doctrines require *the assent of theological faith* by all members of *the* faithful. Thus, whoever obstinately places them in doubt or denies them falls under the censure of *heresy*, as indicated by the respective canons of the codes of canon law.[12]

6. The second proposition of the *Professio fidei* states: "I also firmly accept and hold each and everything definitively proposed by the Church regarding teaching on faith and morals." The object taught by this formula includes *all those teachings belonging to the dogmatic or moral area,*[13] *which are necessary for faithfully keeping and expounding the deposit of faith, even if they have not been proposed by the Magisterium of the Church as formally revealed.*

Such doctrines *can be defined solemnly by the Roman pontiff when he speaks ex cathedra or by the college of bishops gathered in council, or they can be taught infallibly by the ordinary and universal Magisterium of the Church as a "sententia definitive tenenda."*[14] Every believer, therefore, is required to give *firm and definitive assent* to these truths, based on faith in the Holy Spirit's assistance to the Church's Magisterium, and on the Catholic doctrine of the infalli-

---

[11] Cf. *DS* 3074.

[12] Cf. CIC, cann. 750 and 751; 1364, §1; Code of Canons of the Eastern Churches, cann. 598; 1436, §1.

[13] Cf. Paul VI, *Humanae vitae,* 4: *AAS* 60 (1968), 483; John Paul II, *Veritatis splendor,* 36-37: *AAS* 85 (1993), 1162-63.

[14] Cf. *Lumen gentium,* 25.

bility of the Magisterium in these matters.[15] Whoever denies these truths would be in a position of *rejecting a truth of Catholic doctrine*[16] *and would therefore no longer be in full communion with the Catholic Church.*

7. The truths belonging to this second paragraph can be of various natures, thus giving different qualities to their relationship with revelation. There are truths which are necessarily connected with revelation by virtue of a *historical relationship*, while other truths evince a logical connection that expresses a stage in the maturation of understanding of revelation which the Church is called to undertake. The fact that these doctrines may not be proposed as formally revealed, insofar as they add to the data of faith *elements that are not revealed or which are not yet expressly recognized as such,* in no way diminishes their definitive character, which is required at least by their intrinsic connection with revealed truth. Moreover, it cannot be excluded that at a certain point in dogmatic development the understanding of the realities and the words of the deposit of faith can progress in the life of the Church, and the Magisterium may proclaim some of these doctrines as also dogmas of divine and Catholic faith.

8. With regard to the nature of the assent owed to the truths set forth by the Church as divinely revealed (those of the first paragraph) or to be held definitively (those of the second paragraph), it is important to emphasize that there is no difference with respect to the full and irrevocable character of the assent which is owed to these teachings. The difference concerns the supernatural virtue of faith: In the case of truths of the first paragraph, the assent is based directly on faith in the authority of the word of God (doctrines *de fide credenda*); in the case of the truths of the second paragraph,

---

[15] Cf. *Dei Verbum*, 8 and 10; Congregation for the Doctrine of the Faith Declaration *Mysterium Ecclesiae*, 3: *AAS* 65 (1973), 400–401.
[16] Cf. John Paul II, *Ad tuendam fidem* (May 18, 1998).

the assent is based on faith in the Holy Spirit's assistance to the Magisterium and on the Catholic doctrine of the infallibility of the Magisterium (doctrines *de fide tenenda*).

9. The Magisterium of the Church, however, teaches a doctrine to be *believed as divinely revealed* (first paragraph) or to be *held definitively* (second paragraph) with an act which is either *defining* or *non-defining*. In the case of a *defining* act, a truth is solemnly defined by an ex cathedra pronouncement by the Roman pontiff or by the action of an ecumenical council. In the case of a *non-defining* act, a doctrine is taught *infallibly* by the ordinary and universal Magisterium of the bishops dispersed throughout the world who are in communion with the successor of Peter. *Such a doctrine can be confirmed or reaffirmed by the Roman pontiff, even without recourse to a solemn definition,* by declaring explicitly that it belongs to the teaching of the ordinary and universal Magisterium as a truth that is divinely revealed (first paragraph) or as a truth of Catholic doctrine (second paragraph). Consequently, when there has not been a judgment on a doctrine in the solemn form of a definition, but this doctrine, belonging to the inheritance of the *depositum fidei*, is taught by the ordinary and universal Magisterium, which necessarily includes the pope, such a doctrine is to be understood as having been set forth infallibly.[17] The declaration of *confirmation* or *reaffirmation* by

---

[17] It should be noted that the infallible teaching of the ordinary and universal Magisterium is not only set forth with an explicit declaration of a doctrine to be believed or held definitively, but is also expressed by a doctrine implicitly contained in a practice of the Church's faith, derived from revelation or, in any case, necessary for eternal salvation, and attested to by the uninterrupted tradition: Such an infallible teaching is thus objectively set forth by the whole episcopal body, understood in a diachronic and not necessarily merely synchronic sense. Furthermore, the intention of the ordinary and universal Magisterium to set forth a doctrine as definitive is not generally linked to technical formulations of particular solemnity; it is enough that this be clear from the tenor of the words used and from their context.

the Roman pontiff in this case is not a new dogmatic definition, but a formal attestation of a truth already possessed and infallibly transmitted by the Church.

10. The third proposition of the *Professio fidei* states: "Moreover, I adhere with religious submission of will and intellect to the teachings which either the Roman pontiff or the college of bishops enunciates when they exercise their authentic Magisterium, even if they do not intend to proclaim these teachings by a definitive act."

To this paragraph belong *all those teachings—on faith and morals—presented as true or at least as sure, even if they have not been defined with a solemn judgment or proposed as definitive by the ordinary and universal Magisterium.* Such teachings are, however, an authentic expression of the ordinary Magisterium of the Roman pontiff or of the college of bishops and therefore require *religious submission of will and intellect.*[18] They are set forth in order to arrive at a deeper understanding of revelation, or to recall the conformity of a teaching with the truths of faith, or last to warn against ideas incompatible with these truths or against dangerous opinions that can lead to error.[19]

A proposition contrary to these doctrines can be qualified as *erroneous* or, in the case of teachings of the prudential order, as *rash* or *dangerous* and therefore *tuto doceri non potest.*[20]

11. Examples. Without any intention of completeness or exhaustiveness, some examples of doctrines relative to the three paragraphs described above can be recalled.

---

[18] Cf. *Lumen gentium*, 25; Congregation for the Doctrine of the Faith, "Instruction on the Ecclesial Vocation of the Theologian," 23 and 24: *AAS* 82 (1990), 1559-61.

[19] Cf. "Instruction on the Ecclesial Vocation of the Theologian," 23 and 24.

[20] Cf. CIC, cann. 752, 1371; Code of Canons of the Eastern Churches, cann. 599, 1436, §2.

To the truths of the first paragraph belong the articles of faith of the creed, the various Christological dogmas[21] and Marian dogmas;[22] the doctrine of the institution of the sacraments by Christ and their efficacy with regard to grace;[23] the doctrine of the real and substantial presence of Christ in the Eucharist[24] and the sacrificial nature of the eucharistic celebration;[25] the foundation of the Church by the will of Christ;[26] the doctrine on the primacy and infallibility of the Roman pontiff;[27] the doctrine on the existence of original sin;[28] the doctrine on the immortality of the spiritual soul and on the immediate recompense after death;[29] the absence of error in the inspired sacred texts;[30] the doctrine on the grave immorality of direct and voluntary killing of an innocent human being.[31]

With respect *to the truths of the second paragraph*, with reference to those connected with revelation by a logical necessity, one can consider, for example, the development in the understanding of the doctrine connected with the definition of papal infallibility prior to the dogmatic definition of Vatican Council I. The primacy of the successor of Peter was always believed as a revealed fact, although until Vatican I the discussion remained open as to whether the conceptual elaboration of what is understood by the terms *jurisdiction* and *infallibility* was to be considered an intrinsic part of revelation or only a logical consequence. On the other hand, although its character as a divinely revealed truth was defined

---

[21] Cf. *DS* 301-02.
[22] Cf. Ibid., 2803, 3903.
[23] Cf. Ibid., 1601, 1606.
[24] Cf. Ibid., 1636.
[25] Cf. Ibid., 1740, 1743.
[26] Cf. Ibid., 3050.
[27] Cf. Ibid., 3059–75.
[28] Cf. Ibid., 1510–15.
[29] Cf. Ibid., 1000–1002.
[30] Cf. Ibid., 3293; *Dei Verbum,* 11.
[31] Cf. John Paul II, *Evangelium vitae,* 57: *AAS* 87 (1995), 465.

in Vatican Council I, the doctrine on the infallibility and primacy of jurisdiction of the Roman pontiff was already recognized as definitive in the period before the council. History clearly shows, therefore, that what was accepted into the consciousness of the Church was considered a true doctrine from the beginning and was subsequently held to be definitive; however, only in the final stage—the definition of Vatican I—was it also accepted as a divinely revealed truth.

A similar process can be observed in the more recent teaching regarding the doctrine that priestly ordination is reserved only to men. The supreme pontiff, while not wishing to proceed to a dogmatic definition, intended to reaffirm that this doctrine is to be held definitively,[32] since, founded on the written word of God, constantly preserved and applied in the Tradition of the Church, it has been set forth infallibly by the ordinary and universal Magisterium.[33] As the prior example illustrates, this does not foreclose the possibility that in the future the consciousness of the Church might progress to the point where this teaching could be defined as a doctrine to be believed as divinely revealed.

The doctrine on the illicitness of euthanasia, taught in the encyclical letter *Evangelium vitae*, can also be recalled. Confirming that euthanasia is "a grave violation of the Law of God," the pope declares that "this doctrine is based upon the natural law and upon the written word of God, is transmitted by the Church's Tradition and taught by the ordinary and universal Magisterium."[34] It could seem that there is only a logical element in the doctrine on euthanasia, since Scripture does not seem to be aware of the concept. In this case, however, the interrelationship between the orders of faith and reason becomes apparent: Scripture, in fact, clearly excludes every

[32] Cf. Ibid., *Ordinatio sacerdotalis,* 4: *AAS* 86 (1994), 548.

[33] Cf. Congregation for the Doctrine of the Faith, "Response to a Dubium Concerning the Teaching Contained in the Apostolic Letter *Ordinatio sacerdotalis:*" *AAS* 87 (1995), 1114.

[34] *Evangelium vitae,* 65.

form of the kind of self-determination of human existence that is presupposed in the theory and practice of euthanasia.

Other examples of moral doctrines which are taught as definitive by the universal and ordinary Magisterium of the Church are: the teaching on the illicitness of prostitution[35] and of fornication.[36]

With regard to those truths connected to revelation by historical necessity and which are to be held definitively, but are not able to be declared as divinely revealed, the following examples can be given: the legitimacy of the election of the supreme pontiff or of the celebration of an ecumenical council, the canonizations of saints (dogmatic facts), the declaration of Pope Leo XIII in the Apostolic Letter *Apostolicae curae* on the invalidity of Anglican ordinations. . . .[37]

As examples of *doctrines belonging to the third paragraph*, one can point in general to teachings set forth by the authentic ordinary Magisterium in a non-definitive way which require degrees of adherence differentiated according to the mind and the will manifested; this is shown especially by the nature of the documents, by the frequent repetition of the same doctrine or by the tenor of the verbal expression.[38]

12. With the different symbols of faith, the believer recognizes and attests that he professes the faith of the entire Church. It is for this reason that, above all in the earliest symbols of faith, this consciousness is expressed in the formula *we believe*. As the *Catechism of the Catholic Church* teaches: "*I believe* (Apostles' Creed) is the faith of the Church professed personally by each believer, principally during baptism. *We believe* (Nicene-Constantinopolitan Creed) is the faith of the Church confessed by the bishops assembled in council or more generally by the liturgical assembly of believers. *I believe* is also

---

35 Cf. *CCC,* 193.
36 Cf. *CCC,* 2353.
37 Cf. *DS* 3315-19.
38 Cf. *Lumen gentium,* 25; "Ecclesial Vocation of the Theologian," 17, 23 and 24.

the Church, our mother, responding to God by faith as she teaches us to say both *I believe* and *we believe.*"[39]

In every profession of faith, the Church verifies different stages she has reached on her path toward the definitive meeting with the Lord. No content is abrogated with the passage of time; instead, all of it becomes an irreplaceable inheritance through which the faith of all time, of all believers, and lived out in every place, contemplates the constant action of the Spirit of the risen Christ, the Spirit who accompanies and gives life to his Church and leads her into the fullness of the truth.

Rome, from the offices of the Congregation for the Doctrine of the Faith, June 29, 1998, the solemnity of the Blessed Apostles Peter and Paul.

Joseph Cardinal Ratzinger   Archbishop Tarcisio Bertone
Prefect   *Secretary*

---

[39] *CCC,* 167.

APPENDIX I

■ ■ ■

SOME BRIEF RESPONSES TO QUESTIONS REGARDING THE *PROFESSIO FIDEI*

1. Because the truths of the second paragraph of the *Professio fidei* are described as "definitive" does it follow that these truths can also be described as "irreformable"?

Affirmative.

The word "definitive" was chosen because this is the term used in *Lumen gentium*, no. 25, which speaks of *sententia definitive tenenda*. The word "irreformable," on the other hand, was used in the dogmatic constitution *Pastor aeternus* of the First Vatican Council with regard to dogmatic definitions. There is no essential difference between the two terms with regard to their conceptual substance. At the same time, however, in both cases—that is, regarding irreformable dogmatic definitions and doctrines which are to be held definitively—the Church teaches that, while the meaning and conceptual content must always remain the same, these truths may come to be expressed in language that is more complete and more perfect (cf. Congregation for the Doctrine of the Faith, *Mysterium Ecclesiae*, no. 5).

Text taken from *Proclaiming the Truth of Jesus Christ*. Papers from the Vallombrosa Meeting (Washington, DC: United States Catholic Conference, 2000), 61–66.

2. Is it true that every doctrine which has been set forth definitively must also be considered as having been taught infallibly?

Affirmative.

It would be contradictory for the Magisterium to require, by an act that is not infallible, firm and definitive assent to a doctrine set forth as divinely revealed or as intrinsically necessary for keeping and expounding the deposit of faith. It must be remembered, however, that it is a doctrine of the Church's faith that the Magisterium can teach a doctrine infallibly both by an act that is defining (i.e., in solemn form) or by an act that is not defining (i.e., in ordinary form).

○ The first case is that of an ex cathedra definition by the Roman pontiff or a solemn pronouncement by an Ecumenical Council.

○ The second case is that of a teaching of the ordinary and universal Magisterium, which can be formally reaffirmed or confirmed by the ordinary Magisterium of the Pope (see, e.g., Pope Paul VI's *Credo of the People of God* [1968], the apostolic letter *Ordinatio sacerdotalis,* or the three pronouncements found in the encyclical letter *Evangelium vitae*).

The essential point is that *the Magisterium can teach a doctrine infallibly without necessarily having recourse to the form of a (solemn) definition.*

3. Does the second paragraph of *Professio fidei* correspond to what was previously called "the secondary object of infallibility"?

To respond to this question, some distinctions have to be made. If by the "secondary object of infallibility" is meant exclusively the area of truths of a rational or natural order—as perhaps was maintained by certain currents of the post-Tridentine theology of the manuals—then it is clear that the truths of the second paragraph of the *Professio fidei* go beyond this area and would include other doctrines as well. However, if by the "secondary object of infallibility" is meant the area of doctrines that have a necessary logical or historical connection with divine Revelation, then the answer to the question must be affirmative. Furthermore, the process of dogmatic development illustrates how, in the consciousness of the Church, the understanding of the realities and the words of the deposit of faith can progress to the point where the Magisterium may proclaim some of these doctrines as dogmas of divine and Catholic faith including elements that previously had not been expressly recognized as revealed.

It would be helpful, therefore, to recall that the area of the truths belonging to the second paragraph includes doctrines of various types. They can be described as follows:

o Doctrines concerning faith and morals that the Church holds as definitive, although they have not been expressly and categorically set forth as divinely revealed. This does not exclude the possibility that in the course of dogmatic development the Magisterium could, at a later point, proclaim such doctrines as dogmas of divine and Catholic faith. Examples of these would include the doctrine of the primacy of jurisdiction of the Roman pontiff in the period before the dogmatic proclamation of the First Vatican Council; the impossibility of conferring priestly ordination of women; the sacramentality of the Diaconate and the Episcopate taught at the Second Vatican Council, but not set forth as a dogma of faith; and the doctrines that refer to the universal negative moral norms prohibiting intrinsically evil acts.

o Doctrines or facts that the Church proposes infallibly to be held definitely, even though they are not formally revealed. Examples of these would be the canonization of saints; the judgment on the invalidity of the present rite of

Anglican ordinations, and the legitimacy of a particular ecumenical council. These are based ultimately on faith in the Holy Spirit's assistance to the Church and on the Catholic doctrine of the infallibility of the Magisterium.

○ Doctrines concerning faith and morals, which have been obtained by the addition of true elements—though not formally revealed—to other elements deriving directly from Revelation. Examples would include the condemnation of the positions of Jansen; the teaching of the Council of Constance, which defined as theologically certain the licitness of reception of Holy Communion under only one species; the condemnation of those who believe that the secret confession of sins to a priest is opposed to the teaching of Christ; the anathema of those who would affirm that marital indissolubility, as understood by the Catholic Church, is contrary to the Gospel; and the philosophical possibility of demonstrating the existence of God or the spiritual nature and immortality of the human soul.

The distinction between the two paragraphs, corresponding to the respective orders of truth, does not introduce an addition or an extrinsic quantitative increase of doctrine to the deposit of faith. Rather, it seeks to specify more precisely the different relationships that—within the deposit of the faith—individual doctrines have with the foundation and the center of divine Revelation.

4. Could the teaching of *Ordinatio sacerdotalis* belong to the first paragraph of the *Professio fidei*?

The Doctrinal Commission of the Second Vatican Council explained the text of *Lumen gentium*, no. 25, regarding the object of infallibility in the following words: *"Obiectum infallibilitatis Ecclesiae . . . eamdem habet extensionem ac depositum revelatum; ideoque extenditur ad ea omnia, et ad ea tantum, quae vel directe ad ipsum depositum revelatum spectant, vel quae ad idem depositum sancte custodiendum et fideliter exponendum requiruntur. . ."* (*Acta Synodalia Sacrosancti Concilii Oecumenici Vaticani II,* vol. III, no. 1, 251). This means that the doctrines that relate to the deposit of the faith are not only those that directly belong to it, but also the doctrines necessary for the integral preservation of that deposit.

The difference between the truths of the first paragraph and those of the second is not therefore to be found in the fact that only the first are contained in the deposit of the faith, but rather in the fact that the first, since they are directly revealed, are expressly set forth as such by the infallible Magisterium. The second are set forth infallibly in a definitive way, because they are necessarily connected to divine Revelation either by virtue of a logical or historical relationship. Thus, in the final analysis, the definitive character of such statements (of the second paragraph) derives from Revelation itself.

The doctrine of *Ordinatio sacerdotalis* can be held legitimately by theologians to be a doctrine of divine and Catholic faith (i.e., as belonging to the first paragraph). For the moment, however, the Magisterium has simply reaffirmed it as a truth of the Church's doctrine (the second paragraph), based on Scripture, attested to and applied in the uninterrupted Tradition, and taught by the ordinary and universal Magisterium, without declaring it to be a dogma that is divinely revealed.

Therefore, it is not contrary to the Magisterium to classify this doctrine as a truth of divine and Catholic faith; such a claim is, however, for the moment a theological opinion. On the other hand, it would be contrary to the teaching of the Church to maintain that this doctrine belongs to the third paragraph and as such requires only religious submission of intellect and will, and not a firm and irrevocable assent. For example, before the proclamation of the dogma of the Assumption of the Mother of God, it was legitimate in theology, though not obligatory, to maintain that this teaching was a doctrine that was divinely revealed; but it was not legitimate to cast doubt on the teaching itself or to maintain that it was only a prudential teaching and thus open to revision.

5. Is it possible to hold the position that the Magisterium does not have the capacity to teach infallibly regarding particular applications of the natural moral law?

The instruction *Donum veritatis* (no. 16) of the Congregation for the Doctrine of the Faith states the following:

> By reason of the connection between the orders of creation and redemption, and by reason of the necessity, in view of salvation, of knowing and observing the whole moral law, the competence of the Magisterium also extends to that which concerns the natural law (cf. *Humanae vitae*, 4). Revelation also contains moral teachings which per se could be known by natural reason. Access to them, however, is made difficult by man's sinful condition. It is a doctrine of the faith that these moral norms can be infallibly taught by the Magisterium (cf. *Dei Filius,* chapter 2; *DS* 3005).

So given that the observance of all negative moral norms that concern intrinsically evil acts *(intrinsece mala)* is necessary for salvation, it follows that the Magisterium has the competence to teach infallibly and to make obligatory the definitive assent of the members of the faithful with regard to the knowledge and application in life of these norms. This judgment belongs to the Catholic doctrine on the infallibility of the Magisterium.

With regard to the particular application of the norms of the natural moral law that do not have a necessary connection with Revelation—for example, numerous positive moral norms that are valid *ut in pluribus*—it has not been defined nor is it binding that the Magisterium can teach infallibly in such specific matters.

6. The "Doctrinal Commentary on the *Professio fidei*" states that a person who denies a truth of the second paragraph would no longer be in full communion with the Church. Does it follow from this that such a person cannot be admitted to the sacraments?

Negative.

Ad tuendam fidem chapter 4 (part A) gives the new version of canon 1371, 1° of the Code of Canon Law; it speaks of "a just penalty."

BIBLIOGRAPHY

■ ■ ■

OFFICIAL DOCUMENTS

Abbott, Walter, M., ed. *Documents of Vatican II.* New York: America Press, 1966.

Acta Synodalia Sacrosancti Concilii Oecumenici Vaticani II. Vatican City: Libreria Editrice Vaticana, 1970ff.

Carlen, Claudia, ed. *The Papal Encyclicals, 1740–1981.* 5 vols. Wilmington, NC: McGrath, 1981.

Catechism of the Catholic Church. 2d ed., Vatican City: Libreria Editice Vaticana, 2000.

Congregation for Bishops. *Apostolorum successores. Directory for the Pastoral Ministry of Bishops.* Vatican City: Libreria Editrice Vaticana, 2004.

Congregation for the Doctrine of the Faith. *Mysterium Ecclesiae.* "Declaration in Defense of the Catholic Doctrine of the Church Against Certain Errors of the Present Day." *Origins* 3 (1973): 97, 99–100, 110–12.

———. Declaration *Inter Insigniores.* "Women in the Ministerial Priesthood." *Origins* 6 (February 3, 1977): 517, 519–24.

———. "Profession of Faith." Origins 18 (March 16, 1989): 661, 663.

———. *Donum veritatis.* "Instruction on the Ecclesial Vocation of the Theologian." *Origins* 20 (July 5, 1990): 117, 119–26.

———. "Response to *Dubium.*" *Origins* 25 (November 30, 1995): 401, 403–5

Dupuis, Jacques, ed. *The Christian Faith in the Doctrinal Documents of the Catholic Church.* 6th ed. Staten Island, NY: Alba House, 1996.

John Paul II. Apostolic Exhortation *Catechesi tradendae.* "On Catechetics." *Origins* 9 (November 8, 1979): 329, 331–48.

———. Apostolic Constitution *Sapientia Christiana.* "Norms for Ecclesiastical Universities and Faculties." *Origins* 9 (June 7, 1979) 33, 35–45.

————. Apostolic Letter *Ordinatio sacerdotalis.* "On Ordination and Women." *Origins* 24 (June 9, 1994): 49, 51–52.

————. Encyclical *Evangelium vitae.* "The Gospel of Life." *Origins* 24 (April 6, 1995): 689, 691–727.

————. Apostolic Letter *Apostolos suos.* "The Theological and Juridical Nature of Episcopal Conferences." *Origins* 28 (July 30, 1998): 152–58.

————. Apostolic Letter *Ad tuendam fidem.* "To Defend the Faith." *Origins* 28 (July 16, 1998): 113–16.

————. Apostolic Exhortation *Pastores Gregis.* "Shepherds of the Flock." *Origins* 33 (November 6, 2003): 353, 355–92.

National Conference of Catholic Bishops. *The Challenge of Peace: God's Promise and Our Response. A Pastoral Letter on War and Peace.* Washington, DC: United States Catholic Conference, 1983.

————. *Economic Justice for All. Pastoral Letter on Catholic Social Teaching and the U.S. Economy.* Washington, DC: United States Catholic Conference, 1986.

————. "The Teaching Ministry of the Diocesan Bishop: A Pastoral Reflection." *Origins* 21 (January 2, 1992): 473, 475–92.

Paul VI. Encyclical *Mysterium fidei,* 1965. In Carlen, *Papal Encyclicals,* 5:165–77

————. Encyclical *Humanae vitae,* 1968. In Carlen, *Papal Encyclicals,* 5:223–36.

Pius XII. Encyclical *Humani generis,* 1950. In Carlen, *Papal Encyclicals,* 4:174–84.

————. Encyclical *Fidei donum,* 1957. In Carlen, *Papal Encyclicals,* 4:321–32.

Pontifical Council for Justice and Peace. *Compendium of the Social Doctrine of the Church.* Vatican City: Libreria Editrice Vaticana, 2005.

Synod of Bishops. "The Final Report." *Origins* 15 (December 19, 1985): 444–50.

Tanner, Norman. *Decrees of the Ecumenical Councils.* 2 vols. Washington, DC: Georgetown University Press, 1990.

UNOFFICIAL PUBLICATIONS

Alberigo, Giuseppe. *Lo Sviluppo della dottrina sui poteri nella Chiesa universale.* Rome: Herder, 1964.

—————, et al., ed. *The Reception of Vatican II*. Washington, DC: The Catholic University of America Press, 1987.

Bacht, Heinrich. "Sind die Lehrentscheidungen der ökumenischen Konzilien göttlich inspiriert?" *Catholica* 13 (1959): 128–39.

Balthasar, Hans Urs von. "Theology and Sanctity." In his *Word and Redemption*, 49–86. Essays in Theology 2. Montreal: Palm, 1965.

Baraúna, Guilheme, ed. *L'Église de Vatican II: Études autour de la Constitution conciliaire sur l'Église*. Vols. 2–3. Unam Sanctam 51b and 51c. Paris: Cerf, 1966.

Beal, John P., James A. Coriden, and Thomas J. Green, ed. *New Commentary on the Code of Canon Law*. New York: Paulist, 2000.

Brown, Raymond E., Joseph A. Fitzmyer, and Roland E. Murphy. *The New Jerome Biblical Commentary*. Englewood, NJ: Prentice Hall, 1990.

Cano, Melchior. *De locis theologicis* (1562). Reprinted in *Theologiae cursus completus*. Vol. 1 (Paris: J. P. Migne, 1839), cols. 58–715.

Cartechini, Sisto. *Dall'Opinione al Domma: Valore delle Note teologiche*. Rome: Civiltà Cattolica, 1953.

Chicago Studies, vol. 17 no. 2 (1978). Theme issue: The Magisterium, the Theologian, and the Educator. Contributions by J. L. Bernardin, R. E. Brown, Y. Congar, A. Dulles, E. LaVerdiere, J. E. Lynch, C. J. Peter, and others.

Clément, Olivier. *You Are Peter: An Orthodox Theologian Reflects on the Exercise of Peter's Primacy*. Hyde Park, NY: New City Press, 2003.

Colson, Jean. *L'Épiscopat catholique: Collégialité et Primauté dans les trois premiers siècles de l'Église*. Paris: Cerf, 1963.

Congar, Yves. *Sainte Église: études et approches ecclésiologiques*. Paris: Cerf, 1963.

—————. "En guise de conclusion." In Baraúna, *L'Église de Vatican II*, 3:1365–73.

—————. *Tradition and Traditions: An Historical and a Theological Essay*. New York: Macmillan, 1966.

—————. "Origines d'une trilogie ecclésiologique à l'époque rationaliste de la théologie." Translation from Josef Fuchs with commentary, *Revue des sciences philosophiques et théologiques* 53 (1969): 185–211.

—————. *Vraie et fausse Réforme dans l'Église*. 2d rev. ed. Unam Sanctam 72. Paris: Cerf, 1969.

————. *L'Église: une, sainte, catholique, et apostolique.* Mysterium Salutis, vol. 15. Paris: Cerf, 1970.

————. *L'Église de S. Augustin à l'époque moderne.* Paris: Cerf, 1970.

————. *Ministères et communion ecclésiale.* Paris: Cerf, 1971.

————. "Reception as an Ecclesiological Reality." In *Election and Consensus in the Church,* edited by Giuseppe Alberigo and Antonius Weiler, 43–78. Concilium 77. New York: Herder and Herder, 1972.

————. "Theologians and the Magisterium in the West: From the Gregorian Reform to the Council of Trent." *Chicago Studies* 17 (1978): 210–24.

————. "A Semantic History of the Term 'Magisterium'." In Curran and McCormick, *The Magisterium and Morality,* 297–313.

————. "A Brief History of the Forms of the Magisterium and Its Relations with Scholars." In Curran and McCormick, *The Magisterium and Morality,* 314–31.

————. *The Meaning of Tradition.* San Francisco: Ignatius, 2004.

Curran, Charles E., and Richard A. McCormick. *The Magisterium and Morality.* Readings in Moral Theology No. 3. New York: Paulist, 1982.

Di Berardino, Angelo and Basil Studer. *A History of Theology.* Vol. 1: *Patristic Period.* Collegeville, MN: Liturgical Press, 1996.

Dionne, J. Robert. *The Papacy and the Church: A Study of Praxis and Reception in Ecumenical Perspective.* New York: Philosophical Library, 1987.

Dulles, Avery. *A Church to Believe In.* New York: Crossroad, 1982.

————. "An Ecclesial Model for Theological Reflection: The Council of Jerusalem." In *Tracing the Spirit: Communities, Social Action and Theological Reflection,* edited by James E. Hug, 218–41. New York: Paulist, 1983.

————. *The Reshaping of Catholicism.* San Francisco: Harper & Row, 1988.

————. *Models of Revelation.* New York: Doubleday, 1983; reprinted Maryknoll, NY: Orbis, 1992.

————. *The Assurance of Things Hoped For: A Theology of Christian Faith.* New York: Oxford, 1994.

————. "Synod of Bishops." In *The New Dictionary of Catholic Social Thought,* edited by Judith A. Dwyer, 930–32. Collegeville: MN: Liturgical Press, 1994.

————. *The Craft of Theology.* 2d ed. New York: Crossroad, 1995.

Dupré la Tour, François. *Le Synode des Évêques et la Collégialité.* Malesherbes, France: Parole et Silence, 2004.

Empie, Paul C., et al., ed. *Teaching Authority and Infallibility in the Church.* Lutherans and Catholics in Dialogue 6. Minneapolis: Augsburg, 1980.

Eno, Robert B. "Some Elements in the Pre-history of Papal Infallibility." In Empie et al., *Teaching Authority and Infallibility in the Church,* 238–58.

Eynde, Damien van den. *Les normes de l'enseignement chrétien dans littérature patristique des trois premiers siècles.* Paris: Gabalda, 1933.

Faith and Order: Louvain 1971. Faith and Order Paper No. 59. Geneva: World Council of Churches, 1971.

Fiorenza, Francis S. "The Church's Religious Identity and Its Social and Political Mission." *Theological Studies* 43 (1982): 197–225.

Fitzmyer, Joseph A. "The Office of Teaching in the Christian Church according to the New Testament." In Empie et al., *Teaching Authority and Infallibility in the Church,* 186–212.

Fransen, Peter. "The Authority of Councils." In John M. Todd, ed., *Problems of Authority,* 43–78. Baltimore: Helicon, 1962.

Hercsik, Donath. *Die Grundlagen unseres Glaubens: Eine theologische Prinzipienlehre.* Münster: Lit Verlag, 2005.

Kern, Walter, ed. *Die Theologie und das Lehramt.* Quaestiones Disputatae 91. Freiburg: Herder, 1982.

———— and F. J. Niemann. *Theologische Erkenntnislehre,* 2d ed. Düsseldorf: Patmos, 1990.

————, Hermann J. Pottmeyer, and Max Seckler, ed. *Handbuch der Fundamentaltheologie.* Vol. 4, 2d ed. Tübingen: A. Francke, 2000.

Küng, Hans. *Structures of the Church.* New York: Nelson, 1964.

Latourelle, René. *Theology of Revelation.* Staten Island, NY: Alba House, 1966.

LaVerdiere, Eugene A. "The Teaching Authority of the Church: Origins in the Early New Testament Period." *Chicago Studies* 17 (1978): 172–87.

Lerch, Joseph. "Teaching Authority in the Church (Magisterium)." In *New Catholic Encyclopedia* 13:959–65. New York: McGraw-Hill, 1967.

Lécuyer, Joseph. "La triple charge de l'évêque." in Baraúna, *L'Église de Vatican II,* 891–914.

Lehmann, Karl and Semmelroth, Otto. *Theses on the Relationship between the Ecclesiastical Magisterium and Theology,* approved by the International Theological Commission, June 6, 1976. Reprinted in Curran and McCormick, *The Magisterium and Morality,* 151–70.

Löhrer, Magnus. "Träger der Vermittlung." *Mysterium Salutis,* 1:545–87. Einsiedeln: Benziger, 1965.

Lubac, Henri de. *The Splendor of the Church.* San Francisco: Ignatius, 1986.

Lynch, John E. "Apostolic Fathers to Gregorian Reform." *Chicago Studies* 17 (1978): 186–209.

Malloy, Christopher J. *Engrafted into Christ: A Critique of the Joint Declaration.* New York, Peter Lang, 2005.

Metz, Johannes Baptist, ed. *Faith and the World of Politics.* Concilium 36. New York: Paulist, 1968.

Meyer, Harding, ed. *Lutheran/Roman Catholic Discussion on the Augsburg Confession, Documents—1977–1981.* Geneva, Switzerland: Lutheran World Federation, 1982.

Morrisey, Francis G. *Papal and Curial Pronouncements: Their Canonical Significance in Light of the Code of Canon Law.* 2d ed. Ottawa: St. Paul University, Faculty of Canon Law, 2001.

Newman, John Henry. "Letter to the Duke of Norfolk." Reprinted in Alvan S. Ryan, ed., *Newman and Gladstone: The Vatican Decrees.* Notre Dame, IN: University of Notre Dame Press, 1962.

———. *On Consulting the Faithful in Matters of Doctrine,* ed. John Coulson. Kansas City, MO: Sheed & Ward, 1961, 1985.

———. *An Essay on the Development of Christian Doctrine.* Notre Dame, IN: University of Notre Dame Press, 1989.

O'Connor, James T., ed. *The Gift of Infallibility: The Official Relatio on Infallibility of Bishop Vincent Gasser at Vatican Council I.* Boston: St. Paul Editions, 1986.

One in Christ, vol. 6, no. 3 (1970). Theme issue on Catholicity and Apostolicity with articles by A. Ganoczy, J. N. D. Kelly, E. Lanne, W. Pannenberg, R. Schnackenburg, and others.

Pilarczyk, Daniel E. "The Role of the Theologian in a Catholic College or University in the Light of *Ad Tuendam Fidem* and the *Professio Fidei*." In *Proclaiming the Truth of Jesus Christ: Papers from the Vallombrosa Meeting*, 69–82.

Pottmeyer, Hermann J. "Ecumenical Dialogue and Reception." In *L'Intelletto Cristiano*. Studi in onore di Mons. Giuseppe Colombo, edited by Facoltà Teologica Italia Settentrionale, 359–78. Milan: Glossa, 2004.

Proclaiming the Truth of Jesus Christ: Papers from the Vallombrosa Meeting. Washington, DC: United States Catholic Conference, 2000.

Quinn, Jerome D. "'Charisma veritatis certum': Irenaeus, *Adversus haereses* 4, 26, 2." *Theological Studies* 39 (1978): 520–25.

Rahner, Karl. "The Development of Dogma." In his *Theological Investigations* 1:39–77. Baltimore: Helicon, 1961.

———. *Inspiration in the Bible*. Rev. trans. New York: Herder and Herder, 1964.

———. "Dogmatic Constitution on the Church, chapter 3, arts. 18–27." In *Commentary on the Documents of Vatican II*, edited by Herbert Vorgrimler, 1:186–226. New York: Herder and Herder, 1967.

Ratzinger, Joseph. *"La collégialité épiscopale, développement théologique."* In Baraúna, *L'Église de Vatican II*, 3:763–90.

———. *Principles of Catholic Theology*. San Francisco: Ignatius, 1987.

———. "The *Catechism of the Catholic Church* and the Optimism of the Redeemed." *Communio: International Catholic Review* 20 (1993): 469–84.

———. *The Nature and Mission of Theology*. San Francisco: Ignatius, 1995.

———. *"Stellungnahme."* *Stimmen der Zeit* 217 (1999): 169–71.

———. *Pilgrim Fellowship of Faith: The Church as Communion*. San Francisco: Ignatius, 2005.

Ratzinger, Joseph, and Tarcisio Bertone. "Commentary on the Profession of Faith's Concluding Paragraphs." *Origins* 28 (July 16, 1998): 116–19.

Rusch, William G. *Reception: An Ecumenical Opportunity*. Philadelphia: Fortress, 1988.

Salaverri, Ioachim. *De Ecclesia Christi,* in Michaele Nicolau et al., ed., *Sacrae Theologiae Summa,* vol. 1, 3d ed. (Madrid: Biblioteca de Autores cristianos, 1955), 497–988.

Santogrossi, Ansgar. *Vers Quelle Unité? Un oecuménisme en quête de cohérence.* Paris: Éd. Hora Decima, 2005.

Scheeben, Matthias-Joseph. *Handbuch der katholische Dogmatik.* Freiburg: Herder, 1873.

Schnackenburg, Rudolf. "Apostolicity: the Present Position of Studies." *One in Christ* 6 (1970): 243–73.

Seckler, Max. "Kirchliches Lehramt und theologische Wissenschaft. Geschichtliche Aspekte, Probleme und Lösungselemente." In Kern, *Die Theologie und das Lehramt,* 17–62.

Sokolowski, Robert. *Christian Faith and Human Understanding.* Washington, DC: The Catholic University of America Press, 2006.

Sullivan, Francis A. *Magisterium: Teaching Authority in the Catholic Church.* New York: Paulist, 1983.

———. *Creative Fidelity: Weighing and Interpreting Documents of the Magisterium.* New York: Paulist, 1996.

———. "Some Observations on the New Formula for the Profession of Faith." *Gregorianum* 70 (1989): 552–54.

———. "Infallible Teaching on Moral Issues? Reflections on *Veritatis Splendor* and *Evangelium Vitae.*" In *Choosing Life: A Dialogue on Evangelium Vitae,* edited by Kevin W. Wildes and Alan Mitchell, 77–89. Washington, DC: Georgetown University Press, 1997.

———. *From Apostles to Bishops: The Development of the Episcopacy in the Early Church.* New York: Newman, 2001.

Thils. Gustave. *L'Infaillibilité pontificale.* Gembloux: Duculot, 1969.

Tomko, Jozef, ed. *Sinodo dei Vescovi: Natura, Metodo, Prospettive.* Vatican City: Libreria Editrice Vaticana, 1985.

Ullmann, Walter. *Medieval Foundations of Renaissance Humanism.* Ithaca, NY: Cornell University Press, 1977.

Vincent of Lerins. *Primum Commonitorium.* Patrologia latina, col. 637–86.

Walgrave, Jan. *Unfolding Revelation.* Philadelphia: Westminister, 1972.

Wojtyla, Karol. *Sign of Contradiction.* New York: Seabury, 1979.

GENERAL INDEX

■ ■ ■

INDEX TO
SCRIPTURAL CITATIONS

INDEX OF
CANON LAW CITATIONS